THOMAS COO
Travelle

CW00368886

FLORIDA

BY
DOREEN TAYLOR-WILKIE

Produced by AA Publishing

Written by Doreen Taylor-Wilkie

Edited, designed and produced by AA Publishing.
Maps © The Automobile Association 1993

Distributed in the United Kingdom by AA Publishing,
Norfolk House, Priestley Road, Basingstoke, Hampshire,
RG24 9NY.

The contents of this publication are believed correct at the
time of printing. Nevertheless, the publishers cannot accept
responsibility for errors or omissions, or for changes in the
details given in this guide or for the consequences of any
reliance on the information provided by the same.
Assessments of attractions, hotels, restaurants and so forth
are based upon the author's own experience and, therefore,
descriptions given in this guide necessarily contain an
element of subjective opinion which may not reflect the
publishers' opinion or dictate a reader's own experiences on
another occasion.

**We have tried to ensure accuracy in this guide, but things do
change and we would be grateful if readers would advise us of any
inaccuracies they may encounter.**

First published 1993
Revised second edition © The Automobile Association 1995
© The Automobile Association 1993

A CIP catalogue record for this book is available from the British
Library.

ISBN 0 7495 0944 9

Published by The Automobile Association (a trading name of
Automobile Association Developments Limited, whose registered office
is Norfolk House, Priestley Road, Basingstoke, Hampshire RG24 9NY.
Registered number 1878835) and the Thomas Cook Group Ltd.

Colour separation: BTB Colour Reproduction, Whitchurch, Hampshire

Printed by Edicoes ASA, Oporto, Portugal

Cover picture: *St Petersburg beach*
Title page: *a taste of things to come*
Above: *fun in the sun*

Contents

Introduction

*F*lorida is what you make it. It is silver-gold beaches lined with sabal palms, or busy beaches where musclemen practise their attitudes, and the volleyball is fast.

Florida is the blue of the Atlantic, the emerald of the Gulf of Mexico, the golden sunsets of the west and the Keys, alligators and brilliant coloured birds. Florida is the skyscrapers of downtown Miami.

The best-known face of Florida is the bright lights, theme parks, the excitement of the waves and stomach-churning thrill rides of Orlando. And for many visitors Florida is Disney – bringing to life all those wonderful characters from childhood.

For the visitor who likes sport, watersport, any sport, Florida is a chain of endless golf courses, small boat harbours, fishing piers, bright coloured sails and ocean-going cruisers, or the tiny tube of the snorkeller bobbing just above the surface of the buoyant sea.

Florida is also history. Within its boundaries are the two oldest European settlements in America, dating back to the 16th century, long before the Pilgrim Fathers reached the continent. Yet, modern Florida is young and did not become a state until 1845. Perhaps that accounts for its zest for life.

Key West, the most southerly of the Keys, is vibrant and hectic, but its beaches, like those of all the islands, are perfect for the more relaxing pursuits of fishing and boating

THOMAS COOK'S FLORIDA
Florida has increased in popularity – so much so in recent years that it is worth noting that Thomas Cook, as early as 1885, was advertising it as a winter resort for his US clients and for travellers from Britain. This was only possible because of the railroad that had recently been opened by Henry Flagler.

FLORIDA QUOTES

'Florida has a mood, you know. She is young, she is animated, she has sparkle and "go".'
Rex Beach, *The Miracle of Coral Gables*, 1926

'As I went farther and farther north ... I found that more and more people lusted toward Florida ... the very name Florida carried the message of warmth and ease and comfort. It was irresistible.'
John Steinbeck (Pulitzer- and Nobel-prize winner), *Travels with Charley*, 1962

'The garden of America, may her terraces and foundations, her statuary and promenades be margined by fruits of literature and morality.'
19th-century Independence Day Toast to Florida

'Florida ... does beguile and gratify me – giving me my first and last sense of the tropics, or à peu près, the subtropics...'
Henry James, *Letter to Edmund Gosse*, 1905

'In Florida, through sitting and gazing at Nature, I gradually learnt the way which I should eventually find myself.'
English composer Frederick Delius (1862–1934)

'Miami Beach is a rich sandbar with a drawbridge, and in no sense part of the main.'
Gore Vidal, *Reflections upon a Sinking Ship*, 1969

White sands and surf typical of the beaches at Fort Lauderdale

'Behold him rushing forth from the flags and reeds. His enormous body swells. His plaited tail brandished high. The waters like a cataract descend from his opening jaws, clouds of smoke issue from his dilated nostrils. The earth trembles with his thunder ...'
William Bartram, naturalist-explorer, on seeing an alligator fight. *Travels*, 1791

'The commodities of this land are more than are yet knowen to any man: for besides the land itself, whereof there is more than any king Christian is able to inhabit, it flourisheth with medow, pasture ground, with woods of Cedar and Cypres, and others sorts, as beter can not be in the world.'
Voyage of Sir John Hawkins, 1565

History

Some 8,000 to 10,000 years ago, long before any European saw Florida, Indians had settled here and, when the first Spaniards arrived in the 16th century, they found Apalachee and Timucuan Indians living in communities, with family and social structures and religions.

1513
The Spaniard Ponce de León lands near present-day St Augustine on 2 April, looking for Bimini.

1539–59
More Spanish exploration: Hernando de Soto and 600 men in the west near Tampa, and Tristan De Luna, who forms a colony near Pensacola, but has to withdraw after a hurricane.

1564–65
French Huguenots build Fort Caroline on the St John's river, and Spain's Philip II sends Pedro Menéndez de Avilés to capture the fort and found St Augustine for Spain.

1702–04
After a 52-day siege, the British capture St Augustine, though the Castillo remains intact.

1763–83
Florida becomes British, then Spanish again by 1783.

1813
Governor Andrew Jackson captures Pensacola during a series of Spanish-American border conflicts.

1818
First Seminole War between the local Seminole Indians and the US Army.

1821
Jackson receives title to the Floridas from Spain, in Pensacola.

1822
A unified government is established under Governor William P Duval.

1823
Tallahassee is selected as seat of the new government.

1834–37
Start of Florida's first railroad operations.

1835–37
Second Seminole War, with two US Army companies massacred and the Indian leader Osceola imprisoned.

1845
Florida becomes the 27th state admitted to the Union.

1861
Florida withdraws from the Union to fight for the Confederacy during the American Civil War.

1864
Battle of Olustee, which is won by the Confederate troops.

1865
Home Guards and Cadets save Tallahassee from capture by Federals.

But by 20 May the Union flag flies once more over Tallahassee's Capitol.

1868
A new Constitution grants equal suffrage to all races.

1880s and 1890s
Henry Flagler and Henry Plant build their luxury hotels and railroads.

1894–99
The Great Frosts.

1898
The Spanish-American War turns Florida into a huge embarkation camp.

1914
The world's first scheduled airline service, St Petersburg–Tampa.

1935
A hurricane destroys the Keys Overseas Railroad, killing some 400 people.

1961
First American astronauts launch into space from Cape Canaveral.

1965
Announcement that Walt Disney World is to be built at Orlando.

1969
The first manned moon landing by Apollo 11.

1971
Magic Kingdom opens, the first theme park at Florida's Walt Disney World.

1977
Severe frost devastates the citrus groves (also in 1983).

1981
First manned Space Shuttle flight from Kennedy Space Center.

1983
First American woman astronaut, Sally Ride, is launched in *Challenger*.

1992
Hurricane Andrew hits the east coast of Florida.

Aldrin on the moon with the US flag

Geography

*T*he wide plateau that forms Florida is one of the most stable areas in the world, and little has happened since it took its present shape millions of years ago.

The state is also one of the flattest in the US. Its highest hill near Lakewood in the northeast is just 345 feet, hardly big enough to merit a name. Other places in peninsular Florida, such as the Everglades, rise no higher than 10 feet above the sea.

The Floridian Plateau is flat-topped and low lying, extending in a series of gently graduating terraces into the Atlantic Ocean and the Gulf of Mexico. Throughout its long history, the peninsula has been alternately covered in water or poking its top out of the sea as water levels have changed. Over millions of years, this has built up a sediment of limestone over the old rock, two miles thick in the south, which helped to form the Keys and the coral reefs around them.

Sunsets over Key West are spectacular. Just before the sun sinks below the horizon the natural phenomenon of a 'green flash' can often be seen

Diverse landscapes

So close to the ocean, Florida may have more to worry about than most on the subject of global warming. However, the changing water levels have formed such rare and wonderful landscapes as the Everglades and Big Cypress National Preserve. The area's rainfall also keeps water draining south, first into Lake Okeechobee, then further south into the Everglades to form mangrove swamps near the sea and, inland, the slow-moving sawgrass 'River of Grass'.

In its varied geography, Florida might have been designed for pleasure and open-air pastimes. What could be better for safety and ease of sailing and boating than the barrier islands that form the Intracoastal Waterway? The great rivers and thousands of lakes provide space for watersports and fishing, and the beaches are endless, broad stretches of either gold or almost white sand, ideal for fishing and scuba diving, some with salt marshes which attract interesting birdlife. There are also hundreds of springs, wonderful outpourings of the purest water, gushing out a massive 100 cubic feet per second.

The vegetation is certainly lush enough to merit the name of *La Florida* ('flowery'). Florida has flora and fauna characteristic of both temperate zones and the sub-tropics. Its flora ranges from the tropical 'hammocks' (mini-jungles) of West Indian hardwood trees, to pines thriving on more open land.

Sunlight and sea breezes

Florida is nicknamed the 'Sunshine State' and this is borne out by a steady 80-81°F in mid-summer down to 52°F in a northern winter. The Keys rarely drop below 70°F. Most of the rain comes in summer but the brief heavy

The Everglades, haunt of alligators

daily showers are a blessing after the uncomfortable humidity, as are the cooling breezes from the sea.

Hurricanes occur in Florida, with June to November being the peak hurricane season. Most recently, and most spectacularly, Hurricane Andrew slammed into Florida's east coast just south of Miami, doing an estimated $20 billion in damage, killing at least 22, and leaving thousands homeless. Although the state has learned from past disasters, the force of this storm, and the possibility that global warming may contribute to the development of even more lethal storms, should cause the state to re-evaluate its standards of hurricane preparedness.

Politics

*T*he head of the United States is the President, elected every four years by an Electoral College made up of state representatives. Unlike a constitutional monarch, the President holds the principal executive power.

Tallahassee's domed Capitol building

The legislature, Congress, has two houses. These comprise a 435-member House of Representatives elected every two years and the 100-member Senate, which runs for a term of six years. The two main parties are Democrats and Republicans and it is by no means always the case that the President is of the same party as the majority of Congress.

This Federal side of the United States is divided into 50 states and the District of Columbia, which holds the capital, Washington. Two states are detached from the main body, Alaska and Hawaii. Each state has its own smaller version of the Federal structure. Florida became the 27th state in 1845, and runs its own internal affairs.

Tallahassee was chosen as capital of the newly-joined East and West Floridas in 1823 and the first Legislative Council met there in November 1824 in three log cabins. A beautiful Capitol building with traditional dome was raised in 1845, ready for Florida's confirmation of full statehood. Today, this is overshadowed by a huge 20th-century tower, head-quarters of the present administration. Its 22nd-floor observatory guarantees the best possible view of the plantation country and rolling hills of northern Florida.

During the legislative sessions of Florida's own House of Representatives (120 members) and Senate (40 members), the Capitol is alive with law-making and politics but the bulk of a member's work, as it is throughout the United States, is done in a series of committees.

Florida's supreme power lies with the Governor who, like the President, can serve only two consecutive terms of four years. His official residence is a beautiful Georgia-style Southern mansion, The Hermitage, which is full of 18th- and 19th-century furniture and *objets d'art*. It is open to the public and the gardens are particularly beautiful when the giant magnolias are in bloom.

The Governor is assisted by a Cabinet. They are elected independently, and may well know more about how Florida works than the Governor, because their tenure of office is unlimited. They can be re-elected time and time again.

Finally, Florida today is divided into 67 counties and independent city authorities, which exercise a good deal of power. At one time, there were only two Florida divisions – East and West. After

The billiard room at Whitehall, Henry Flagler's Palm Beach mansion

their union, US Representative Andrew Jackson created two more, St Johns and Escambia, holding the old Spanish cities, St Augustine and Pensacola respectively. Over the years, their number of divisions has steadily risen to the current 67.

Some counties were named after people who had made a significant contribution to the state: Flagler County after the railroad tycoon, Henry Flagler; Osceola after the Seminole leader, imprisoned when he came to a US camp under a flag of truce; and Broward after the quaintly named Napoleon Bonaparte Broward, the 19th Governor.

Culture

*I*t is a paradox that Florida, America's southernmost area, is not one of the Southern States – certainly not in the *Gone with the Wind* tradition of plantation houses, cotton, and mint juleps on the open porches. You will have to cross the border into Georgia and Alabama to find these vestiges of the past.

A Miccosukee Indian village

Florida is a northern state in a southern position, with a population largely made up of Northerners moving south. The main reason is that Florida was not settled in the same way as the Southern States. It has the continent's oldest European community, St Augustine, but the influence there was Spanish.

Between 1775 and 1782, as the American colonies to the north were fighting their own War of Independence, Florida was coming to the end of a 20-year period under British rule, and was handed back to Spain by the British at the end of that war. In turn, American independence brought British settlers from the North who had opted against becoming American.

In the 19th century, the native Indians fought three fierce wars (the Seminole Wars) against the new state of Florida and though, at the end, some 4,000 Seminoles were deported north, many remained. Some retreated to remote areas such as the Everglades until well into this century. (Today's Miccosukee Indians, who live around the Tamiami Trail and Alligator Alley, are descendants of the Seminoles.) The end of the Civil War also brought freedom to the slaves.

At the southern end of the peninsula, the Spanish influence was and is still strong, all along the Keys. Most notable are the many Cuban immigrants who worked in the cigar industry, first in Key West, then in Tampa.

Despite this, Florida was largely virgin land until the railroad came. Henry Flagler laid rails down the length of the east coast, Henry Plant made

The Venetian Pool at Coral Gables

tracks on the west coast (though only as far as Tampa). With the 'Iron Horse' came new settlers, and holiday visitors too. As the railroad moved south, so did they. The land boom of the early 1920s increased the population from a mere handful of 55,000 in 1845 to just under a million, in 1920, and by half as much again, to 1½ million in the decade that followed.

During that time, every architect's ambition was to design a Florida district, such as Miami's Coral Gables (one of the first planned garden cities in America). Here, the developer George Merrick had a vision of a group of 'villages', each in a different style, with strict controls on design and dimensions. This near-fantasy atmosphere was popular and may have influenced the style of today's theme parks. Innovative ideas brought in new people, and many monied people. Florida's population is now over 13 million. But there is nothing static about it. For every two

who move into Florida as new residents, one leaves.

Today, many newcomers are different in that they have moved north to Florida, from Cuba, the Caribbean, and Latin America. This is a whole new type of Floridian, bringing a culture, cuisine, and a way of life that many Northerners have adopted with delight.

Florida life is leisurely. The climate ensures that. There is also the endless pursuit of sport and outdoor social occasions. It is a little like the Mediterranean spiced with American 'go'. Unlike the past, most people now live in cities, not because they moved in from the land but because they came direct to fast-growing communities.

To the visitor the most obvious characteristic that has come out of this pot-pourri of cultures is how casual people are. There is never any need for formality in Florida.

First Steps

*T*here's no hard and fast rule for dividing Florida into areas but this is the order in which the book introduces the Sunshine State.

IN AND AROUND ORLANDO

This is the heart of the man-made world of theme parks and film studios, with Disney and Universal managing to combine the two. In and around Orlando, there is every kind of family entertainment from exciting wild-water parks, to hot-air balloons, museums and dining attractions, all with a theme designed to make them different. Among the high-tech fantasy worlds, however, are plenty of reminders that the early Central Floridians were cattle ranchers and citrus growers, working on the land. Springs, forests, rivers and lakes still enhance the quality of life out of doors.

Daytona Beach: these days the famous sands are usually covered with cars

THE ATLANTIC EAST COAST

The Atlantic east coast stretches from Ormond Beach and Daytona Beach, the first Millionaire's Row and the 'birthplace of speed', south to today's Millionaire's Row at Palm Beach, and on to Fort Lauderdale. In between is the Space Coast, home of space flight since the first unmanned satellites in 1958. Yet, here, alongside the high-tech spacecraft of the Kennedy Space Center, is an unspoilt wild coast, full of natural beauty.

GREATER MIAMI AND ITS BEACHES

Downtown Miami is a city of the 21st century, all glass and metal reaching for the sky. Greater Miami is also a collection of communities, each with its own style: Coconut Grove, bohemian but smart; George Merrick's Old World – Coral Gables; and Opa-Locka, a feat of imagination from the *Arabian Nights.* Miami Beach, reborn as the Art Deco capital of the world, is, of course, world-famous for its sands. Miami has entertainment galore with museums, sports and gardens. It swings by night, and has a unique culture as the gateway to the Americas further south.

THE KEYS

The Keys are also unique, some 100 miles of coral reefs and islands from Key Largo to Key West. Each key is different; some quiet, some bubbling. All

are perfect places to be on, or even
better, under the water, investigating the
cool depths. Key West's tempo can be
fast or slow, with a daily celebration of
the sunset down at the waterfront.

THE SOUTHWEST GOLD COAST

This is the coast of a 'Thousand
Islands', from Marco Island (the largest)
in the south, to Anna Maria Island in the
north, just before the wide entrance to
Tampa Bay. Many of the islands and
much of the coast have exquisite
beaches, where the pace of life is never
hurried.

PINELLAS, TAMPA AND
ST PETERSBURG

Tampa Bay was known to the Spaniards
as early as the 1530s, when Hernando de
Soto sailed in. Now, its beautiful waters
are crossed by the Sunshine Skyway
Bridge. St Petersburg, at the southern

Miami's revived Art Deco quarter

end of the Bay, is a green, open city with
wide streets and a famous pier. The
Pinellas has some of the best seaside
coastline in Florida. The area is in the
happy position of being close to the sea,
yet only a couple of hours from
Orlando's hectic attractions.

THE NORTH

From St Augustine to Pensacola –
Florida's two oldest communities – the
north stretches along the area known as
the Panhandle, and the Emerald Coast.
Tallahassee, the state capital, lies like an
oasis in the heart of rolling hills – the
nearest thing Florida has to the Old
South. Jacksonville, on the east coast, is
the main gateway in and out of the state.
For Europeans, this is the least known
area of Florida, but it is worth extending
a trip to travel north.

Getting Around

*T*he USA is the land of the automobile and Florida is no exception. A car is absolutely essential here and will take you almost anywhere in just a few hours. Public transport is a low priority in most areas and is unsuitable for getting around the tourist sites efficiently.

By car

A car gives you freedom to come and go, and petrol (or 'gas') is gratifyingly cheap by European standards. Outside the cities, roads are usually good, wide, and not too full except on public holidays. Downtown can be a confusing nightmare because Americans use their cars even for the shortest of journeys.

The Orlando skyline behind the Interstate

By air

Florida has a strong internal network of flights. In addition to the three international airports, Miami, Tampa and Orlando, more than a dozen main regional airports provide flights to link the state. There are also many smaller airfields, useful for getting to remoter places.

Off-peak internal flights can cost not much more than a train or bus fare, much less usually than the British or European equivalent. Independent travellers should explore the Visit USA scheme which gives around 30 per cent discount on a full-priced US domestic ticket (though an off-peak, once you're there, may be cheaper) and the US Air Pass coupon schemes operated by main US airlines in Britain (and British Airways in association with USAir) which must also be bought before you leave. Enquire, and compare prices.

By train (Amtrak)

There's something exciting about a train that you know is going nearly 1,500 miles all the way from Miami to New York. The big train is clean and comfortable, with excellent on-board service.

Though the railroad's turn-of-the-century glory has gone, the Amtrak train enters (and leaves) Florida at Jacksonville, comes south through

Orlando (with a side route to Tampa) and on via West Palm Beach, Fort Lauderdale and the east coast to end at Miami. This makes a leisurely route for overseas visitors who want to take in Orlando and Miami, plus a taste of the beaches. Amtrak also runs some connecting bus services. For independent travellers heading north after Florida, an Amtrak saves a lot of driving, as well as giving a chance to see the scenery in comfort. Amtrak's Eastern Regional Railpass includes Florida (and the whole of eastern North America from Montreal to Chicago and New Orleans in the west).

Also investigate the Greater Miami Metrorail (overhead railroad). Designed for commuters, this can be useful for seeing some of the sights of Greater Miami South.

By bus
Bus travel is the cheapest way (though not spectacularly so) of getting around. Long-distance buses mean Greyhound, with frequent services between main centres and towns. However, between remoter communities they are limited to a few times a week. Unless you are constantly on the move, or take a bus out of Florida after a visit, a Greyhound Ameripass (bought before you leave) is scarcely worthwhile. The Greater Miami area has cheap, though not fast, local buses for southeast coast travel. For detailed information on getting about, see the **Practical Guide.**

THE WAY OF LIFE
Almost without exception, people you meet in Florida are straightforward and ready to be friendly. Hospitality at home is likely to be very informal, often a supper on the verandah or a visit to a

boat either to sail or sit on deck. Floridians are also great eaters-out, and friends may meet for a meal in one of the dozens of restaurants downtown.

Language
One of the advantages for the English-speaking visitor to Florida ought to be the fact that Americans speak the same language, but it's the sort of easy assumption that could lead to confusion. The two languages may sound much the same apart from the accent, but many words have different, and sometimes subtly different, meanings. For example, never say someone is 'homely', it means 'ugly' – the proper American equivalent is 'homey'.

In southern Florida, especially Miami, it is not uncommon to see signs in Spanish and English, and many staff in large hotels and restaurants are Spanish-speaking.

The motor car
Think of the terminology of the motor car (automobile), as you take it for petrol (gas). Bonnets are hoods and the boot is a trunk and you don't take your caravan (trailer) off the road on to a lay-by, it's a turn-out.

When to go

July and August tend to be the peak tourist seasons. Queues are long and beaches busy. To avoid the crowds, early November would be a good month to travel as this is not particularly a holiday season in Florida.

What to wear

Florida informality extends very much into the realm of dress and what you

Loose, comfortable clothing is the order of the day everywhere

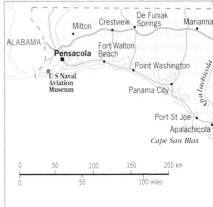

should and should not wear. Informal dress is acceptable year round, and only some of the most exclusive of hotels and restaurants insist on a collar and tie for dining, though a jacket is often no hardship because the air conditioning can be cool. For women, it's a good idea to carry a light wrap when dining, just in case.

From April to September, the weather is mild and warm, so you will only need very lightweight sports clothes, cottons and beachwear. Most hotels prefer you not to come through the lobby in swimsuits, and nude bathing is rare and always signposted. Nobody bothers about young children.

From October to March, the same type of clothes still applies in the central and southern areas but, in the north, a woollen suit, sweater or top coat will sometimes be needed, almost certainly in the evening, and sometimes then in the south, too. At any season, a light raincoat is handy. When the showers come, they are short but usually sharp.

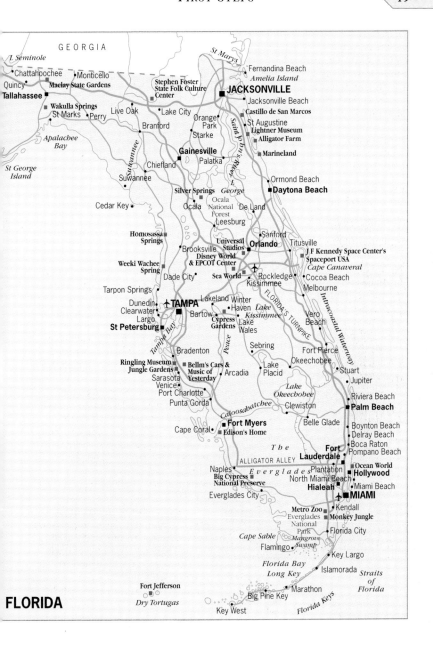

FLORIDA

FLAGS AND EMBLEMS

Many flags have flown over Florida soil: from French to Spanish, to British then back to Spanish, the Stars and Stripes of the United States, not to mention Confederate, Patriot and Mexican colours. However, with only a minor change since 1900, Florida's state flag has been a red diagonal cross on a white background, with the Seal of State at its centre.

Perhaps it was this variety of flags which gave Florida a taste for emblems, ranging from State Beverage to State Song. Stephen C Foster's *The Swanee River,* (usually known as the *Old Folks at Home*) is the State Song, in tribute to the Suwannee River which flows south from Georgia to the Gulf of Mexico, slicing off the Panhandle from peninsular Florida.

A few years earlier, in 1927, the lively mockingbird became Florida's State Bird. Look for this grey-white bird, carolling in spring.

Orange juice and orange blossom as the State Beverage and State Blossom respectively, are no surprise. The blossom has been an

Oranges and orange blossom –
State Beverage and State Blossom

The sabal palm – State Tree

emblem from 1909, and since World War II the prosperous orange juice industry has brought millions of dollars into the economy.

The moonstone, as the State Gem, honoured the 1969 moon landing by Neil Armstrong and 'Buzz' Aldrin, and was a tribute to all the astronauts and workers at the east coast's Kennedy Space Center.

The tall, elegant sabal palm, featured against a blazing sunset on many tourism posters, became State Tree in 1970. A few years later the manatee was chosen as the State Marine Mammal and the porpoise as the State Saltwater Mammal.

The most recent state symbol is the rare Florida panther. This handsome cat, long-tailed and pale brown, is down to around 30 specimens. It was awarded its title in 1982, perhaps in a last-ditch attempt to save it from extinction.

The manatee – State Marine Mammal

The mockingbird – State Bird

Around Historic St Augustine

St Augustine is unique in Florida in managing to preserve so much of its past, and its narrow, pretty streets, some of which are pedestrianised, are ideal for walking. *Allow at least 2 hours.*

Nearby

Oldest Drug Store

Museum Theater

Start at the old City Gate at the north of St George Street.

1 CASTILLO DE SAN MARCOS

The wooden gate and walls, built against the British, were burnt down in 1702. The present gates, made from coquina (a mix of cement and shells), and a stretch of wall below the fort were reconstructed in 1808. Climb up to the ramparts to see how splendidly placed the Castillo is to command the wide Matanzas River and the seaway to the town (see page 120).

Walk south along the seafront, where horses and carriages wait for passengers, towards the Bridge of Lions.

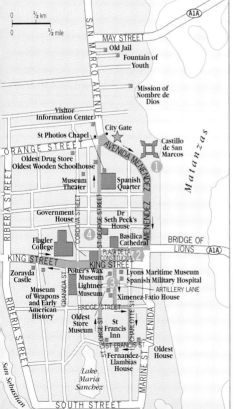

2 PLAZA DE LA CONSTITUCION

This square, complete with its central open market, is a perfect Spanish plaza. To the north is the Basilica Cathedral of St Augustine; west is Government House with a new history museum. Walk over to King Street on the south side and turn right. The imposing building with shady gardens and fountains is the Lightner Museum (see page 122). Opposite is Flagler College, once Henry Flagler's Ponce de León Hotel and now, as a private college (university), still all Spanish Revival architecture and palms. Behind the Lightner Museum in Granada Street is the Antique Mall, in what was the hotel's indoor pool. Further along King

Florida's oldest house, González-Alvarez

Street are the Museum of Weapons and Early American History and the Zorayda Castle, a re-creation of part of the Alhambra Palace in Spain.
Return along King Street to Avilés Street.

3 EARLY RESIDENTIAL DISTRICT

On the corner of Avilés Street is the Potter's Wax Museum, opposite the Lyons Maritime Museum. Further on you come to the Spanish Military Hospital with scents and sights that reflect hospital life for an 18th-century soldier. Crossing Artillery Lane, look right for the Oldest Store Museum, and then as you reach the Cadiz Street crossing, you see the Ximenez-Fatio House, built in 1797, and in 1855 opened by Miss Louise Fatio as a popular boarding house. By the time you turn left into Bridge Street, then right into Charlotte Street, you will have seen many old houses with overhanging balconies and lush gardens. On the corner with St Francis Street are the coquina shellstone walls of St Augustine's Oldest House. Also here are the Fernandez-Llambias House, which has both Spanish and Minorcan heritage, and the town's oldest

inn, the St Francis, built in 1791.
Return towards the Plaza via St George Street. (At Bridge Street a sign indicates that the pink house opposite was owned by Napoleon's nephew, Prince Murat.) Cross the Plaza to rejoin St George Street.

4 ST GEORGE STREET

This pedestrianised street is full of character and crossed by other tempting streets. On your right after the cathedral is Dr Seth Peck's House, dating back beyond 1750, once the Old Spanish Treasury and later the British Governor's residence. Further on is the Spanish Quarter, eight 250-year-old Spanish houses in lovely gardens, with craftworkers and guides in period dress. Next door is St Photios Chapel, the earliest National Shrine of the Greek Orthodox Church in America. It is dedicated to the first settlement at New Smyrna near Daytona (1768), many of whose colonists migrated to St Augustine in 1777. On the left is the Oldest Wooden Schoolhouse, complete with tableaux of pupils and schoolmaster.
A few yards more to the end of the street, and you are back at the City Gate.

A Stroll on Daytona Beach

This short stroll (just under 2 miles) takes in Daytona Beach's famous Boardwalk, Pier, and the wide stretch of creamy sand that saw early racing cars flashing past at record-breaking speeds – the start of Daytona's love affair with everything on wheels. *Allow 2 hours.*

The walk begins in the centre of Daytona Beach at Ocean Pier.

1 OCEAN PIER

From the pier, look out over the rolling Atlantic and down to the beach, which stretches for some 23 miles. In keeping with its past, there is always a line of parked cars, and one or two more moving along at today's 10mph speed limit. Beach-cruiser bicycles, with their noticeable yellow tyres, are available for hire.

Start with a ride up the Pier's Space Needle, circling up to a view that stretches forever – the long beach, lined with hotels and low-rise buildings against endless Atlantic blue, dotted with coloured sails and boats.

Try a gondola ride to the end of the pier and back, high over the dedicated anglers who stand like statues until the sudden shout of 'Got something!' Back to earth, the main pier building was a casino in the 1920s and some of its elegant old

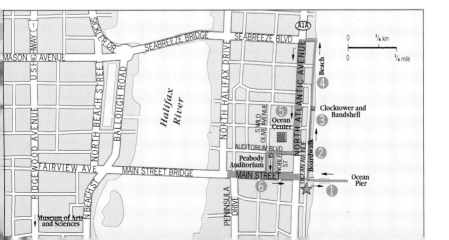

mirrors are still *in situ*. The best place for a coffee stop is the outside platform where you can watch the bustle of beach volleyball, or a pelican spectating from a nearby post (see page 55).
Descend and turn on to the Boardwalk.

2 THE BOARDWALK

The Boardwalk was at its height in the 1930s, and period frontages still remain. Souvenir shops, piled high, sell everything from hot dogs to beach towels, and the Boardwalk's park has miniature golf, arcades and snack food (see page 55).
Stroll along the Boardwalk.

3 THE CLOCK TOWER AND THE BANDSHELL

Daytona gained fame as a testing ground for turn-of-the-century car engines, when pioneers such as R E Olds and Henry Ford not only tested but raced their cars along the beach at the (then) death-defying speeds of over 50mph. In 1935 Sir Malcolm Campbell set the fastest time ever recorded on the beach – 276.8mph, breaking his own record for the fifth time. The clock tower commemorates this event.

The Bandshell also goes back to the 1930s and provides free weekly summer concerts, and many events throughout the year.
At the Bandshell, walk down the steps and on to the beach.

4 THE BEACH

At low tide the beach stretches for some 500 feet to the edge of the sea, its smooth sand ideal for beach games and family picnics (and in March noisy bands of students!). The sea is always warm enough for swimming, surfing and scuba diving.

Soaking up the sun on Daytona Beach

Continue north on the beach and turn left at the underpass at Seabreeze. You're actually walking under Daytona's oldest hotel, built in 1888, now the Howard Johnson. Turn left on to the A1A (Atlantic Avenue). Your target is the sleek white building up ahead.

5 THE OCEAN CENTER AND PEABODY AUDITORIUM

The huge, modern Ocean Center is used for conventions, conferences and sport. Turn right on to Auditorium Boulevard for the Peabody Auditorium, home of the Daytona Beach Symphony Society, Daytona Ballet, classical concerts, and Broadway musicals.
From the Peabody walk along either Noble Street or S Wild Olive Avenue to Main Street.

6 MAIN STREET

This is an old restored area but, in early March, Main Street will be lined on both sides with the world's biggest, shiniest, most modern motor bikes, in town for Motorcycle Week, the bikers' festival. Along here are several famous bikers' bars, such as the Boot Hill Saloon.
Walk seawards on Main Street, back to the Pier.

Around Old Key West

Key West is the tip of mainland United States. Measuring some four miles wide and a couple of miles across, it is full of history and boasts many famous people (see pages 94–7). *Allow 2 hours.*

Nearby

Turtle Kraals

Southernmost House

West Martello Tower

Begin at the sea end of Duval Street. On the right is the sightseeing boats' quay but leave that for later. Cross over Duval and walk down Front Street.

1 MALLORY SQUARE/WATERFRONT

This is the Conch Tour Train terminus. There are several small shops, an excellent aquarium, the Shell Warehouse and Sponge Market. To the seaward side is the Waterfront, famous for sunsets.

Across the road, in the triangle to landward of the red-brick

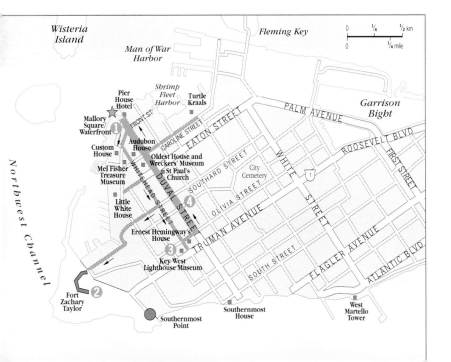

Customs House (built in 1852, and the oldest US Navy building in this important base), is the Mel Fisher Treasure Museum. It is stuffed full of fabulous finds brought up from Spanish treasure ships. Tucked behind the museum is President Truman's summer home on Front Street, known as Harry Trueman's Little White House Museum. Opposite the Mel Fisher Museum on Whitehead Street is Audubon House, where the naturalist and bird artist, John James Audubon, painted during his visit.

At Mallory Square the big pelicans lumber past and the boats speed by and you can watch the comings and goings of this maritime island. If you plan your walk to end just before sunset, this is the best time to enjoy the happy spirit of Key West's celebration of the sunset. *Walk south along Whitehead Street. Past the imposing Post Office, turn right into Southard Street and walk towards Fort Zachary Taylor.*

2 FORT ZACHARY TAYLOR

The fort was an important Union Army stronghold during the Civil War, one of a chain of four covering Key West and the Dry Tortugas, 70 miles to the west. There is a museum which relates the history of the fort.
Back heading south on Whitehead Street, the next stop is Key West's tallest point.

3 KEY WEST LIGHTHOUSE

Don't be put off climbing to the top by the 100 or so steps of Key West Lighthouse. Your reward is a wonderful panorama of the islands and sea, spread out below. The museum at the foot of the lighthouse covers the history of the building. Opposite is Ernest Hemingway's House. He was the first of many writers to discover Key West and

there is lots of fascinating *memorabilia* for his fans.
As you come out of Hemingway's House, turn right and then right again for the short walk to turn left into Duval Street.

Scrimshaw work in Duval Street

4 DUVAL STREET

Apart from places to shop, eat, and drink, Duval Street has food for the spirit too, in St Paul's Episcopal Church on your right. Look inside at its wonderful stained glass. On the left the Oldest House and Wreckers' Museum was once home to a sea captain with nine daughters.

Caroline Street offers a detour to Turtle Kraals, with loggerhead turtles on show, Land's End Marina, and the Shrimp Fleet Harbor.
Back on Duval Street, continue to Front Street. Turn left and walk through to The Waterfront and Mallory Square.

A Stroll along Winter Park's Avenue

Winter Park is a little of New England right in the heart of Florida. Founded by wealthy 19th-century winter visitors, it has kept its small-town charm. Downtown is really just a single street, Park Avenue, with shady trees, white walls, balcony flower boxes and striped awnings over the small shops and cafés. Here the emphasis is on the arts with museums and galleries.

Allow at least 2 hours.

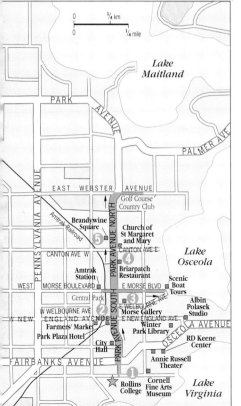

Start at Rollins College at the southern end of Park Avenue.

1 ROLLINS COLLEGE

This is Florida's oldest college, founded in 1885. Take time to look at the beautiful Mediterranean-style buildings, one of which is home to the Cornell Fine Arts Museum. The gardens lead down to Lake Virginia, with a wide view from the museum's patio. Exhibitions change every six weeks with some 2,000 items to call on. Concerts are held in the Cornell Galleries, while the Annie Russell Theater stages an ambitious summer repertory series, and the Knowles Chapel is host to an annual Bach festival.

Window shopping north along Park Avenue reveals almost as many art galleries as shops, and interesting specialists include the old postage stamp shop. Past the City Hall on the left is the Park Plaza Hotel, built in 1922 and featuring an acclaimed restaurant. Behind it, a short walk down W New England Avenue, is the open-air

Saturday morning Farmers' Market (7am–noon), bustling and bright with fruit, flowers and vegetables.

2 CENTRAL PARK

Next comes Central Park and its bandstand, much used during the March Winter Park Festival. It's hard to miss the cheeky squirrels; look out also for Albin Polasek's fountain statue, _Emily_. The Amtrak train stops at the tiny station here, and is part of the mighty route from Miami to New York. The park was a gift to the town from Charles Hosmer Morse, also commemorated in Morse Boulevard, which bisects Park Avenue.

3 MORSE GALLERY

The Morse Gallery, one block further south in E Welbourne Avenue, is world famous for its collection of stained glass by Tiffany (see page 48).

Continue down Morse Boulevard, crossing Interlachen Avenue, for a view of Lake Osceola. Scenic boat tours with a commentary given by a talkative 'skipper' leave from here. They last around one hour and give a unique view of the lakes, inter-connecting canals, and elegant lakeside homes.

4 BRIARPATCH RESTAURANT

Back on Park Avenue, just round the corner, is Vin's Restaurant, with original Tiffany glass. Also along this stretch is the Briarpatch Restaurant where over breakfast you'll see everyone from the County Commissioner to an academic from Rollins College.

5 BRANDYWINE SQUARE

Central Park continues north of Morse Boulevard and, on the left, Brandywine Square has been attractively renovated.

Shops stand round a square with flowers and fountains, open-air cafés and the Brandywine Delicatessen, which boasts 40 different kinds of sandwich. A little further along on the right is the sunny-coloured Roman Catholic Church of St Margaret and Mary, with a handsome stained-glass wall. Walk on past the shady green of the Golf Course Country Club.

Turn right into East Webster Avenue for the Club House, then back to the Avenue.

Louis Tiffany's exquisite art nouveau work can be seen at the Morse Gallery in Park Avenue. This stained-glass lamp features his distinctive dragonfly design

Miami Beach and Art Deco

Miami Beach first shot to fame in the 1920s, when enterprising developers hired talented architects to create buildings in a colour-washed mixture of the Art Deco and Mediterranean Revival styles. After many years of boom and bust the district decayed and was then rescued from decline in the late 1970s, when it was designated a National Historic District. This tour covers the one square mile of the Art Deco district and begins at the even older district of South Pointe. *Allow 2 hours.*

Nearby

Tiffany's Hotel
(spectacular at night)

Essex House

To reach South Pointe from Miami, cross the MacArthur Causeway (US–395) and turn right into Alton Road.

1 SOUTH POINTE PARK

The park is the place to fish and watch the great liners heading through Government Cut to the Port of Miami, the world's largest cruise ship port. Sit outside and enjoy the seafood at Southe Pointe Seafood House.
From the park head north for Biscayne Street.

2 JOE'S STONE CRAB RESTAURANT

This famous restaurant is a fourth-generation, family-run original, established in 1913. The meal to choose is stone crab, mustard sauce, garlic spinach and hash browns. There's no booking so arrive early to get a table. (The restaurant is closed mid-May to mid-October when stone crabs are out of season.)
Walk north on Ocean Drive with the park between you and the sea.

3 OCEAN DRIVE

Visitors soon have their Art Deco
District favourites here. Stroll along
looking at the renovated fantasy styles of
the 1920s and 1930s, with their
decorative columns, arched doors,
wonderful colours, and good restaurants
and porch cafés. Notice the remarkable
Beach Patrol Headquarters at no 1001,
built on the lines of the Art Deco French
liner *Normandie*. All along Ocean Drive,
Lummus Park to the right has been
beautified at a cost of over $2 million,
with a new boardwalk, landscaping and
the planting of some 125 palms.

Two of the most famous buildings
are the Cardozo, the building in the old
1959 Frank Sinatra film *A Hole in the
Head,* and the Leslie Hotel.

*After you pass the Betsy Ross Hotel and just
before Ocean Drive ends, turn left and walk
a block to Collins Avenue. Head north along
Collins Avenue, turn left on to Lincoln
Road, and cross Washington Avenue.*

4 LINCOLN ROAD MALL

This pedestrian area has lots of
interesting Art Deco. Look out for the
Sterling Building's curious tiling effect,
and the Colony Theater's parapet roof
with carved panels, and courtyard
fountain. It was restored in 1986, and is
a frequent venue for ballet, theatre, and
classical music. The Miami Beach
Community Church was the area's first
church and features ornate cherubs and
dolphins. The Mall has many speciality
shops and restaurants.

*By way of Meridian Avenue (which bisects
Lincoln Road), head north for Dade
Boulevard, and the Holocaust Memorial on
the connecting corner.*

5 HOLOCAUST MEMORIAL

This painfully moving museum is a
reminder of some of human history's
darkest years (see page 82). Just behind
it, the Miami Beach Garden and
Conservatory is a good place for
reflection afterwards.

*Return down Meridian Avenue, then turn
left into Española Way. Just before, if
you're not desperate to sit down, walk one
more block to see the newly restored Aloha
Apartments, priced at $20,000 each even
in 1937.*

Tiffany's Hotel in Miami

6 ESPAÑOLA WAY

The gas-lit, cobbled street of Española
Way is a little like being in old Spain,
and has many restaurants, indoors and
out. This is the place to end a tour and
rest your feet. If the view seems familiar,
it's because Española Way has often
been used as a set for *Miami Vice*.

*Return to South Pointe Park along
Ocean Drive.*

Around Fort Lauderdale

Fort Lauderdale is a city famous for its beach, its canals and waterways. It is bounded on the ocean side by the A1A, which stretches from the north to the south of Eastern Florida, rarely far out of sight of the sea. *Allow a day.*

Nearby

Historical Society

Museum

Discovery Center

Start off the tour on the A1A, at the busy Bahia-Mar Yacht Center.

1 BAHIA-MAR YACHT CENTER

You can see all kinds of yachts here, from tiny sailing craft to luxury deep-sea cruisers, complete with enormous catches of grouper, snapper and dolphin (the fish, not the mammal).
Take the A1A (17th St Causeway) south, then left into Eisenhower Boulevard.

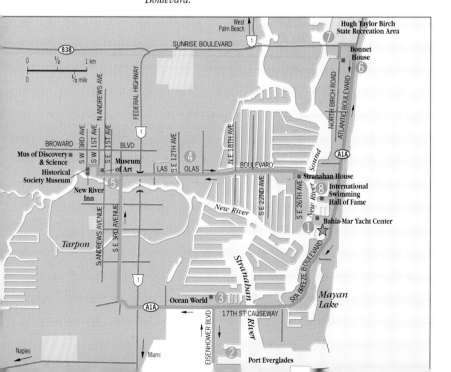

2 PORT EVERGLADES

Here are some of the most sophisticated cruise liners in the world. You can sample some of them on special one-day cruises which visit either the Bahamas or simply cruise in a circle without putting into port. The other stars of the Port are the manatees, winter visitors lured in by the creek's warm water, courtesy of the electricity generating company here. They have a voracious herbivorous appetite so take a head of lettuce to feed them. Exotic reef fish also swim here during winter.

Return to Eisenhower Boulevard and cross 17th St Causeway for Ocean World.

3 OCEAN WORLD

Famed for its Dolphin Show, sea lions, sharks and exotic birds, this is a delight for all the family (see page 67).

Follow 17th St Causeway west across US1, turn right along SE 3rd Avenue and right again on to Las Olas Boulevard. Park the car north of Las Olas shops to see 'Old Fort Lauderdale'.

4 LAS OLAS BOULEVARD

This Spanish-Colonial-style street is famous for fashion, jewellery, art, antiques and good restaurants. Arrive in style for evening dinner by horse and carriage. You'll find Stranahan House, the oldest in the county (built 1901), by turning into Stranahan Place.

Walk west on Las Olas Boulevard as far as SE 3rd Avenue area.

5 MUSEUM OF ART

On the corner with Las Olas Boulevard, the museum has two fine collections: Modern European, and ethnographic, including American Indian. Cross S Andrews Avenue beside the New River

to SW 3rd Avenue for the Historical Society Museum which shows the area from pioneer days to the 1940s. This period is also brought to life in the 1907 King Cromartie House and the historic New River Inn on SW 2nd Avenue – all part of the Himmarshee Village historic district covering eight blocks. The new Museum of Discovery and Science, with its huge IMAX theatre (see page 67) is great fun for all the family with ingenious hands-on exhibits for children.

Return to your car on Las Olas Boulevard, head east over the Causeway to the A1A, and turn left (north). At Sunrise Boulevard, turn left and left again on to North Birch Road.

6 BONNET HOUSE

This was the 1920s home of Frederick Clay Bartlett, and comprises 30 lovely rooms full of art and decorative art. The 35-acre gardens, full of sub-tropical plants, can also be toured by surrey (see page 66).

Go back to Sunrise Boulevard for the entrance to the Hugh Taylor Birch State Recreation Area.

7 HUGH TAYLOR BIRCH STATE RECREATION AREA

This 180-acre park between the Atlantic Ocean and the Intracoastal Waterway is full of interesting wildlife; excellent for picnics and renting canoes.

Head south again on the A1A for the Bahia-Mar Yacht Center.

8 INTERNATIONAL SWIMMING HALL OF FAME

One block away from the Yacht Center, the hall has medals and trophies of 300 famous swimmers from Johnny Weissmuller onwards.

St Petersburg

At weekends, St Petersburg, a city of a quarter of a million inhabitants, can be a quiet contrast to the lively Pinellas beaches. The wide streets make easy driving and there are few parking problems. *Allow a day.*

Nearby

Crescent Lake

Mirror Lake

Start by driving east from the beaches (except St Pete's) by Treasure Island Causeway, which becomes Central Avenue, to 3rd Street. Turn left (north) to 5th Avenue N and left again. This leads right away to 4th Street N. Turn right for Sunken Gardens. From St Pete's Beach, take the Pinellas Bayway east (toll) to I–275. Take I–275 north to I–375, then I–375 east to 4th Street N and turn left for Sunken Gardens.

1 SUNKEN GARDENS

The origin of the name is a sinkhole surrounded by a shallow lake. Around this are five acres of shady, tropical gardens, where 5,000 species of flowers are planted annually. Vivid, exotic birds and animals abound.

Drive south on 4th Street N, to turn left on to 2nd Avenue N. Keep going till you come down to Bayshore Drive, Demens Landing and the busy yacht basins, an area with many car parks.

2 DEMENS LANDING

This lively municipal marina and waterfront park is a pleasant place to stretch your legs. Demens Landing commemorates a Russian emigrant, Peter Demens, co-founder of St Petersburg with General John C Williams, of Detroit. After a Doctor van Bibber made a highly-publicised recommendation that the land had everything that a healthy city required, Demens built his narrow-gauge Orange Belt Railroad and settlers flooded in.

Park the car and walk north along Bayshore Drive.

3 MUSEUM OF FINE ARTS

This Palladian-Mediterranean-style building, just north of the pier through the shady Bayshore Drive gardens, has fine collections of French Impressionists, American and European paintings, and early American photography. Don't miss the Steuben crystal (see page 112).
Walk seawards along 2nd Avenue N towards the pier.

4 ST PETERSBURG HISTORICAL AND FLIGHT ONE MUSEUM

The Historical Museum is the tiny building on the left, which manages to cram in local and state history, with some Egyptian mummies, and changing exhibitions (see page 112).
Complimentary shuttle cars go to the pier but it is a pleasant walk. Don't miss 'Comfort Station No 1', built in 1927. Pier parking for disabled people only.

5 THE PIER

This huge five-storey inverted pyramid has fishing, speciality shops, boat rentals, and a fine view from the fifth-storey restaurant with a lunch-time band. The pink building seen to the right from the pier was once the famous Vinoy Hotel. The toast of the city, it closed its doors in the 1970s and stood empty for 17 years (see page 112).
Return to your car and head west on Central Avenue or 1st Avenue N. Turn left on 4th Street S and left on to 11th Avenue S, to park in any one of three areas.

6 SALVADOR DALI MUSEUM

This superb museum holds the biggest collection of Dali works anywhere. There are 93 oil paintings, 200 watercolours and drawings and over 2,000 *objets d'art* valued at $125 million. A guided tour is highly recommended (see page 112).
Turn left outside the museum and Great Explorations is opposite, diagonally left.

7 GREAT EXPLORATIONS

This is a fascinating hands-on museum, where you can see optical illusions, such as your head on a silver platter! Adults as well as children enjoy the tricky tests of skill and strength (see page 111).
To return to the Pinellas, drive back north along 3rd Street S to turn left at Central Avenue which becomes Treasure Island Causeway. For St Pete's, take 3rd Street north and follow signs to I–275; take I–175 west to I–275, south to Pinellas Bayway, west (toll) back to St Pete's Beach.

Tropical plantlife in the Sunken Gardens

Tampa

Tampa is a busy port and a prosperous commercial and financial centre, with industries such as the famous Anheuser-Busch (Budweiser) brewery and Cuban cigars. It also has a host of fine museums and galleries, and a rich cultural life. *Allow a day.*

From the west, take the Florida Avenue exit (US 41) off South Crosstown Expressway. Head north to Kennedy Boulevard, then left. Cross the bridge and enter the gardens on the right. From the east, come off I–4 west on to I–275 South. Head south on Ashley Drive to Kennedy Boulevard. Turn right and follow directions above.

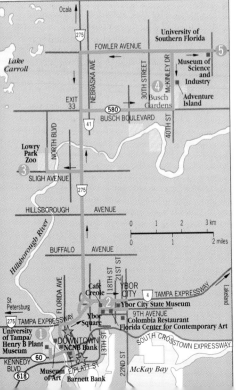

1 UNIVERSITY OF TAMPA-HENRY B PLANT MUSEUM

The astonishing 1891 Moorish building with onion-domed minarets was originally the Tampa Bay Hotel, Plant's answer to Henry Flagler's sumptuous east coast hotels. The university acquired the building in 1933. The museum in the old hotel holds many of Plant's most interesting art and antique treasures gleaned from all over the world.

Don't miss the park's *Sticks of Fire* brushed aluminium sculpture. Walk across the NCNB Bank Plaza to the highly rated Tampa Museum of Art, close to the Hillsborough River. It has, among other works, one of America's best collections of Roman and Greek antiquities.

Head back on Kennedy Boulevard and turn left to Ashley Drive. Continue north to I–275 North exit. Take I–275 North on to I–4, head east to Ybor City exit, south on 21st Street. Turn right on Palm Avenue to 13th Street, and left to Ybor Square.

2 YBOR CITY AND YBOR SQUARE

Café Creole, once the El Pasaje Hotel (1896), at the junction of 14th Street and 9th Avenue, is a good stop for drinks, coffee and desserts. With lovely Spanish-American architecture, it now offers Cajun fare. Ybor Square's three huge buildings, once employing 4,000 19th-century cigar workers, are now a dining and shopping centre, great for Cuban food. The Tampa Rico Cigar Company still hand-rolls cigars.

Preservation Park, on 18th Street, holds six 1890s workers' cottages, one furnished in period style. Another holds the Chamber of Commerce Information Center, which issues leaflets with useful details. Next door Ybor City State Museum gives an excellent background to this colourful suburb.

Seventh Avenue, Ybor City's main street, has many historic buildings, such as the 1917 Ritz Theater, at 15th Street, and the Italian Club dating from 1894, at 18th Street. Opposite is the Florida Center for Contemporary Art.
Back in the car, head east along 9th Avenue, then left on to 22nd Street and drive north until the left turn to I–4 west. Bear off right on to I–275 north. Drive to the Sligh Avenue exit, head west and turn right at North Boulevard.

3 LOWRY PARK ZOO

The animals in this 24-acre zoo live in as near natural conditions as possible. This includes a free-flight aviary with over 65 tropical bird species. There is a manatee research and rehabilitation centre, and a petting area for children.
Drive back east to rejoin the I–275 and head north for two miles to turn off at exit 33 on to Busch Boulevard (SR 580) and drive east for 2 miles to McKinley

The water chute ride – Busch Gardens

Drive (40th Street) and entrance.

4 BUSCH GARDENS

You could take a whole day to explore the turn-of-the century African theme park, with more than 3,000 animals. Koalas are perennially popular, as are the rare white tigers, also bird and dolphin shows. You can also tour these big gardens by train and monorail. Rides include the Python, which loops through 360 degrees. Do buy a plastic coat (on sale) for the Tanganyika Tidal Wave. Children will also enjoy the water theme park, Adventure Island, next door.
Head north on McKinley Drive, turn right on to Fowler Avenue and drive east for a mile.

5 THE MUSEUM OF SCIENCE AND INDUSTRY (MOSI)

This is Florida's largest science centre with over 200 hands-on exhibits including survival in a Gulf Coast hurricane, the Energy Plaza with the country's largest pinball, and Electric Plaza, which will make your hair stand on end.
Drive west along Fowler Avenue to regain I–275, then reverse route to reach down-town Tampa.

North of Orlando

In the busy heart of downtown Orlando, it's hard to remember that, not so long ago, what flourished best in and around this area were citrus fruit and cattle. Yet, even today, it takes little time to drive out to historic small towns, lakes, woods, citrus groves and the great St John's River, once the industrial lifeline to the north. *Allow a day.*

Nearby

Flea World

Big Tree Park

Leave Orlando via I–4 and take exit 51 on to SR–46 East to downtown Sanford and park in any of the central car parks.

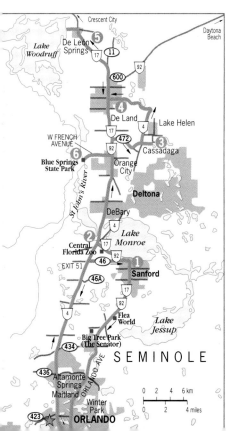

1 SANFORD
Set on the St John's River and Lake Monroe, Sanford is named after the citrus fruit pioneer, Henry Sanford. Its Historic District has 22 'cracker' and Victorian-style buildings on the National Register (the nickname 'cracker' comes from the ranchers' whips, used on cattle drives). There are art galleries, antique shops, booksellers and cafés.
Return to the car and head west some five miles on US17–92.

2 CENTRAL FLORIDA ZOO
Listen out for the unmistakable laugh of the Australian kookaburra and don't miss the cougars in this busy, small zoo.
US17–92 now crosses under I–4, and heads north over the St John's River. Continue some 10 miles to Orange City, and a little further on turn right on to SR 472, then left on to Cassadaga Road, which crosses I–4, following signs for Cassadaga.

3 CASSADAGA
This small village has drawn spiritualists from many places and is now the centre of spiritualism in Florida. If you have a

St John's River, Sanford

taste for fortune telling, a whole host of mediums are eager to give you a reading. Try the Purple Rose Metaphysical Stuff Store, or just enjoy getting a glimpse of old Florida.
Return to I–4 and head north to the junction with SR 44 to DeLand.

4 DELAND

This is the home of Stetson University, which welcomes visitors to look around its fine pillars and porticos. DeLand Hall, facing the main street, is Florida's oldest building of higher education in continuous use, a contrast to the modern Cultural Arts Center opposite, which holds the DeLand Museum of Art. Best of all is the turn-of-the-century Henry Addison DeLand House, just off the main street on W Michigan Avenue. This property displays *memorabilia* connected with the city's founder, dating back to the 1890s.
Continue north on US17–92 (US92 peels off east a few miles north) for nine miles.

5 DE LEÓN SPRINGS

This natural spring pumps out 19 million US gallons a day, and is a marvellous place to swim and canoe. The Old Spanish Sugar Mill, with its huge wooden water wheel, is now a restaurant where you can

make your own pancakes.
Turn back south on US17 and drive to Orange City. Turn right on to W French Avenue and drive two miles west.

6 BLUE SPRINGS STATE PARK

The park was once a port on the St John's river but is now best known as a wintering home for manatees who come here for the constant 72°F waters. The outline of these gentle giants is often clear from the observation platform, and the spring gives good snorkelling.
Back on US17–92, you can either head straight back to Orlando or, after crossing the St John's River (west of Sanford), turn on to I–4 and head back to downtown Orlando.

One of Sanford's well kept streets

Along Florida's First Coast

The historic coast between Jacksonville and St Augustine was home to both the first Spanish and first French settlers and is often titled Florida's First Coast or the Crown. Another name, the Buccaneer Trail (AIA), recalls villains and heroes such as Sir Francis Drake, Jean Lafitte and the feared Blackbeard. Today, the beaches of this fine coast, some 50 miles from Ponte Vedra in the south to Fernandina Beach at the northern-most tip of Florida, have a kinder sort of liveliness. *Allow a day.*

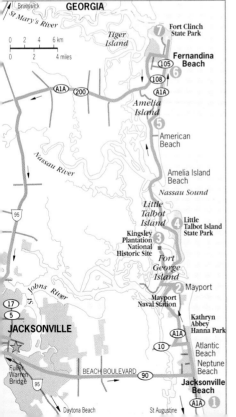

From Jacksonville take the Fuller Warren Bridge, I–95, then almost immediately take SR 90 to Jacksonville Beach, some 20 miles east.

1 JACKSONVILLE BEACH
This is the busiest beach with lots of amenities, and a leaning towards art and artists. On Beach Boulevard are the Beaches Antique Gallery, with more than 120 dealers, and the Pablo Historical Park and Old House Museum, which includes the Station Master's House among its railroad exhibits. On N First Street, the co-operative showroom, Beaches Art and Craft Gallery, shows work by local artists. There is also an American Lighthouse Museum at North Third Street. Heading north, Neptune and Atlantic beaches are good for surfing and, just north again, is the area's favourite, the pure white sands at Kathryn Abbey Hanna Park.
Head north again on A1A.

2 MAYPORT

Mayport Naval Station offers free weekend tours on certain ships and is one of the US Navy's largest home ports. At the mouth of the St Johns River is the 300-year-old fishing village of Mayport with a large shrimp fleet – good for seafood.

Take the Mayport ferry across the St Johns to Fort George Island.

3 KINGSLEY PLANTATION NATIONAL HISTORIC SITE

Built in 1792, this is the oldest surviving plantation house in Florida. This fine old house contrasts with the ruined outbuildings where the slaves lived. Try to fit in the entertaining and informative tour.

Return to A1A and continue north to Little Talbot Island.

4 LITTLE TALBOT ISLAND STATE PARK

The sandy beaches and salt marshes of this barrier island are the place to find river otters, marsh rabbits and bobcats or to try a ranger-led canoe trail for armadillos and more. Nearly 200 bird species have been counted on the island, which also has good swimming.

Follow A1A north.

5 AMELIA ISLAND

One of Amelia Island's claims to fame is that it has lived under eight different flags. The Spanish flag flew here for two periods totalling 236 years; the Patriot flag lasted just one day!

Horseriding is available on the beach. Sea Horse Stables is at the southern tip but you must make a reservation (tel: (904) 261–4878).

Follow A1A to Centre Street (Fernandina Beach).

6 FERNANDINA BEACH (AMELIA ISLAND)

To get a flavour of this historic town, walk down to the shrimp dock, the birthplace of the US shrimping industry. Look out for the Palace Saloon. Built in 1878 and a bar since 1903, it is part Wild West saloon, part Victorian pub. Other notable places are the Marina Restaurant, one of the oldest, Fantastic Fudge, and The Southern Tip. The best way to learn about the area is to take a tour led by guides from the Museum of History on Second Street.

Continue on A1A to the northernmost point.

7 FORT CLINCH STATE PARK (AMELIA ISLAND)

The fort, built in 1847, was designed to protect shipping in the St Mary's River, and was occupied by both Northern and Southern troops during the Civil War. It is seen at its best during the Friday and Saturday summer evening candlelit tours.

The park comprises 1,085 acres and offers good swimming, surf and pier fishing, and a certain satisfaction that you're standing at the very northeastern tip of Florida, above St Mary's Entrance.

Turn south again on A1A and west at SR 200 (still A1A) for the 15-mile-or-so drive to I–95. Turn south on to I–95 for downtown Jacksonville.

Bailey House, with transport at the ready, Amelia Island

In and Around Orlando

*T*he soldiers who fought the Seminole Indians around Orlando would be astonished at what has happened to their old camping ground today, and so would the cattle ranchers and early orange growers who farmed here in the 19th century.

Orlando today is 'New' Florida, a widespread, spacious green city, dedicated to having fun, with theme parks, entertainments, and myriad places to eat. To many it is also synonymous with Walt Disney and the Magic Kingdom, which opened here in 1971. But, even before Disney arrived, some of Orlando's theme parks and fantasy worlds had already been created. Now they are scattered all over Central Florida, a mecca for children and parents alike.

Natural world

This part of Florida is also a natural water world with two great rivers, the Kissimmee and the Peace, and lakes and springs where millions of gallons of the purest water pump out of the ground to form gently turning pools. All are ideal for swimming, fishing and canoeing, and you may even see the great shape of a rare manatee below the surface.

Around Orlando

Orlando is not the only place to enjoy yourself. Other communities, old and new, are within easy reach, each with their own character and things to do and see. Once they were sleepy little places but, as the whole area became more and more popular, gradually they turned into holiday bases, such as Kissimmee/ St Cloud, Ocala, Polk County and Winter Park.

ALLIGATORLAND SAFARI ZOO

Learn all about alligators with more than 2,000 specimens in this zoo park, plus 100 species of other exotic reptiles and animals, including deer, monkeys, big cats and a variety of birds.

4580 W Highway, 192, Kissimmee. Tel: (407) 396–1012. Guided tours. Open: 8.30am–dusk. Admission charge.

APPLETON MUSEUM OF ART

A superb collection of beautifully displayed fine arts, from European paintings, glassware and guns, to pre-Columbian South American, African and Oriental works.

4333 E Silver Springs Boulevard, Ocala (75 miles northwest of Orlando). Tel: (904) 236–5050. Guided tours (advance notice). Open: Tuesday to Saturday 10am–4.30pm, Sunday 1–5pm. Closed: Monday. Admission charge.

ARABIAN NIGHTS

Arabian dancing horses and champion steeds perform in an indoor arena while you tuck into a prime rib dinner (vegetarian, too) in this mock-up palace.

6225 W Irlo Bronson Memorial Highway, Kissimmee. Tel: (407) 239–9223. Reservations required.

BALLOON FLIGHTS

Several companies offer vistas of Central Florida, while you float gently as the sun rises, usually followed by a champagne brunch.

Central Florida Balloon Company, PO Box 2764, Winter Park, Orlando. Tel: (407) 895–1686.

Orange Blossom Balloons, Lake Buena Vista. Tel: (407) 239–7677.

Rise and Float Balloon Tours, 5767 Major Boulevard, Orlando. Tel: (407) 352–8191.

Rosie O'Grady's Balloon Flights, 3529 Edgewater Drive, Orlando. Tel: (407) 841–8787.

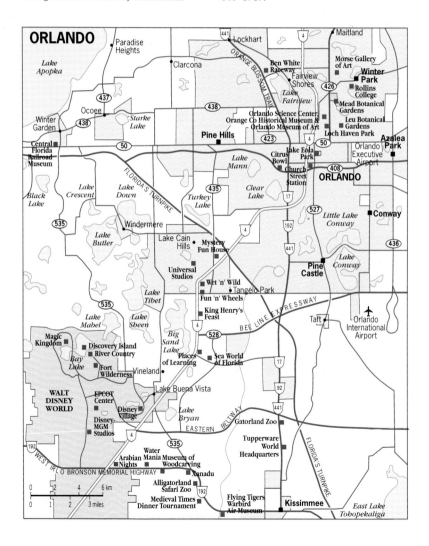

BOK TOWER GARDENS

Open for more than 60 years, these 128-acre gardens contain thousands of gardenias, magnolias, camellias and azaleas. The centrepiece is the famous tower with its 57-bell carillon. Programmes include moonlight recitals.
Burns Avenue and Tower Boulevard, Lake Wales, Polk County. Tel: (813) 676–1408. Open: 8am–5pm. Admission charge.

Doing the can-can at Rosie O'Grady's

CENTRAL FLORIDA RAILROAD MUSEUM

Once the Tavares & Gulf Railroad Depot, the museum's collection of railway *memorabilia* is vast.
101 South Boyd Street, Winter Garden. Tel: (407) 656–8749 or (904) 748–4377. Guided tours. Open: varies (please phone). Sunday: 2pm–5pm. Admission charge.

CHURCH STREET STATION

There really was a station here, and there is still an Historic Train Depot. The theme at Orlando's premier evening entertainment complex spans the decades between the 1890s and the 1920s. The Cheyenne Saloon and Opera House is an old style Western saloon, Rosie O'Grady's is a Louisiana-style bar with can-can girls, and the elegant wrought-iron Orchid Garden is a Victorian Crystal Palace. Antique furnishings and fixtures throughout are of the highest quality, so that each establishment is virtually 'the real thing'. There are other venues where you can hear everything from blue-grass folk to high-energy disco. By day, this attractively renovated depot is a shopping centre with a large number of interesting speciality shops. Eating possibilities are numerous and varied from the expensive restaurant to the sandwich bar.
129 West Church Street, Orlando. Tel: (407) 422–2434. Admission charge to all music venues; free to shopping areas.

CYPRESS GARDENS

The lush 223 acres of these gardens, Florida's longest-established theme park, have two main shows: The Great American Ski Show, and Captain Robin's Flying Circus. Other features include the Botanical Gardens Cruise, the old-time Southern Crossroads and Carousel Cove. Special kids' rides.
SW Orlando off US 19, near Winter Haven. PO Box 1, Cypress Gardens. Tel: (800) 282–2123. Open: 9am–6pm. Admission charge.

FLORIDA CITRUS TOWER

Take the elevator to the top of this 226-foot-high Florida landmark for panoramic views of the citrus groves that brought riches to this pleasant hilly country. Beware, however, that frost damage still mars the landscape. Afterwards take a look at the citrus packing plant, see jams and jellies being made and board the Citrus Grove Tram Tour.

US27 North, Clermont (24 miles west of Orlando). Tel: (904) 394–8585. Guided tours. Open: daily 8am–6pm.

FLYING TIGERS WARBIRD AIR MUSEUM

This World War II (working) flying museum regularly adds new exhibits, all restored to working condition, including a Flying Fortress, a Mustang and a Tiger Moth.

231 N Hoagland Boulevard, Kissimmee. Tel: (407) 933–1942. Guided tours. Open: 9am–5.30pm, Sunday to 5pm.

GATORLAND ZOO

This is the world's biggest alligator farm, with over 5,000 animals, from 9 inches to 15 feet. View them in a native cypress swamp from the walkway or the Gatorland Express. The brave can feed them. A narrow-gauge railroad takes you round the zoo. Snakes, exotic animals and birds are also resident here.

14501 Orange Blossom Trail, Kissimmee, Orlando. Tel: (407) 855-5496. Guided tours (in advance). Open: daily 8am–dusk. Admission charge.

KING HENRY'S FEAST

England's King Henry VIII in royal splendour, celebrating his birthday with a five-course banquet, featuring continuous entertainment with sword swallowers, jugglers, magicians and troubadours.

8984 S International Drive, Orlando.

Henry VIII's birthday is celebrated with feasting and jollities in Orlando

Tel: (407) 351–5151. Open: two shows daily, 6.30pm and 9pm.

LEU BOTANICAL GARDENS

Escape Florida's hot summer sun in the shade of this lush, green 47-acre garden, with scented avenues of roses, camellias, orchids and exotic perennials under flowering trees. The museum features a turn-of-the century lakeside farmhouse, filled with artefacts reflecting the lifestyle of wealthy farmers who cultivated the land between 1910 and 1930.

1730 North Forest Avenue, Orlando. Tel: (407) 246-2620. Guided tours (phone in advance). Open: daily 9am–5pm.

Walt Disney World

*P*eople gather, there's a sudden hush in the music, then the big parade appears. A huge array of floats featuring Mickey, Goofy, Donald and friends passes by, followed by tumblers, dancers and bands, and yet more characters from Disney films.

This is Walt Disney World, the world's biggest tourist attraction. You could spend days, even weeks here, but you should allow a minimum of four days if you are able.

The procession moves past Main Street USA, Disney's childhood memories of small-town America. Along the Street are horse-drawn street-cars and horseless carriages, shops and restaurants, all in an idealised style of days gone by, with jazz musicians and street performers turning each and every day into a celebration. Most children love the Magic Kingdom best of all. It includes 45 major shows and adventures from Pirates of the Caribbean and a headlong ride down Space Mountain to the latest attraction, Splash Mountain. EPCOT has more to offer parents and older children looking not just to the future but also to the culture and architecture of the 11 countries which have opened pavilions on national themes.

A sense of space

On busy days, more than 150,000 eager visitors pour into Disney yet, except when your feet are aching in a queue for a popular attraction, Disney has contrived a sense of space, and byways lead to unexpected corners. Queuing here is a way of life but, if a queue is too long, make for another and return later. Disney fans have even invented queue games to pass the time.

Big as it is, Disney is easy to get around thanks to the transport system. This means the chance to put your car keys in the drawer and turn to the free monorail, buses and ferries.

Drawing up outside Cinderella's Castle

GUIDED TOURS

Open: 9am–closure

by season.

Admission charge.

Lake Buena Vista.

Tel: (407) 824–4321.

A headlong descent of Thunder Mountain

THE MAGIC KINGDOM

What most people think of as Walt Disney World is the Magic Kingdom, a theme park with a permanent festival atmosphere, full of bands, exciting rides, and dozens of children walking past in Donald Duck caps and sporting Mickey Mouse ears. The emphasis here is on the older well-loved characters – Mickey, Donald, Goofy, Cinderella.

DISNEY-MGM STUDIOS

As well as a theme park, Disney-MGM Studios is also a working filmset, and the best introduction is the excellent two-hour Backstage Studio Tour. Here you can see film and television in production, and have a chance to take part. The Animation Tour shows you how cartoons are created, Star Tours sends you on a stomach-churning ride on a *Star Wars* spacecraft, or you can tackle the Tower of Terror ride in the new Sunset Boulevard.

EPCOT

This was Walt Disney's personal dream, and it is sad he did not live to see the great shining geosphere, Spaceship Earth, towering above the entrance. EPCOT Future World is softened science, shown gently by shows, rides, and simulated travel. But EPCOT World Showcase is the place to end the evening, with a top-class international

meal and the grand finale of Illuminations. Against a musical background, each national pavilion is lit up as fireworks explode and lasers pattern the sky – a fitting phantasmagorical end to a fantastic day.

A Disney ticket is expensive but, once inside, it covers everything except the food and souvenirs. There are various types of tickets:
1. Five-day pass for all three big parks covering River Country, Typhoon Lagoon, Discovery Island and Pleasure Island.
2. Four-day passport for all three big parks.
3. One-day ticket allows entry to one theme park.

The huge sphere of Spaceship Earth

MEDIEVAL TIMES AND MEDIEVAL LIFE

Step back nearly a thousand years to a four-course medieval banquet and jousting tournament in an 11th-century 'European' Castle. Visit the adjacent 'medieval' village and take a glimpse of medieval life at work, including a torture chamber.

4510 Irlo Bronson Highway, Kissimmee. Tel: (407) 396–1518. Hours vary, also show times. Admission charge.

Kissimmee's old town quarter

MORSE GALLERY OF ART

A treasure house of Tiffany glass, this personal collection of Hugh and Jeanette McKean contains many pieces rescued at the demolition of Louis Comfort Tiffany's Long Island mansion, Laurelton Hall, to form the world's most comprehensive Tiffany collection, including lamps, stained-glass windows, blown glass, paintings and furniture. It also houses works by Frank Lloyd Wright, Charles Rennie Mackintosh and Lalique and a collection of turn-of-the-century Zanesville pottery (see page 29).

133 E Welbourne Avenue, Winter Park. Tel: (407) 644–3686. Guided tours (phone in advance). Open: Tuesday to Saturday 9.30am–4pm, Sunday 1–4pm. Closed: Monday. Admission charge.

MULBERRY PHOSPHATE FOSSIL MUSEUM

Phosphate miners at Mulberry have unearthed numerous prehistoric fossils. The Mulberry Museum displays many of these fascinating exhibits from the past.

Highway 37 South, Mulberry (32 miles east of Tampa). Tel: (813) 425–2823. Guided tours (reservations). Open: Tuesday to Saturday 10am–4pm.

MYSTERY FUN HOUSE

Explore the mysteries of an Egyptian Tomb in the Forbidden Temple or try out the shooting gallery and miniature golf course in this 15-room fun house. Also features mazes, mirrors and a game room.

5767 Major Boulevard (opposite Universal Studios main gate), Orlando. Tel: (407) 351–3355. Open: autumn to winter 10am–9pm; spring to summer 10am–10pm. Admission charge.

OLD TOWN, KISSIMMEE

The old town has a beautiful roundabout (carousel) with old-fashioned horses and a Ferris wheel, as well as around 70 speciality shops and restaurants, all set in a wash of pastels and ornamental architecture. Go back to the 1950s at Little Darlin's Rock 'N' Roll Palace.

5770 Irlo Bronson Memorial Highway, Kissimmee. Tel: (407) 396–4888. Open: 10am–10pm, year-round.

ORLANDO MUSEUM OF ART

The pride of this museum is its pre-Columbian South American exhibits and African art. The permanent collection includes 19th- and 20th-century

Diamond-backed rattlesnake

American art. There are also changing exhibitions year-round.

2416 North Mills Avenue, Orlando (at Loch Haven). Tel: (407) 896–4231. Guided tours. Open: Tuesday to Thursday 9am–5pm, Friday 9am–9pm, Saturday 10am–5pm, Sunday noon–5pm. Admission charge.

ORLANDO SCIENCE CENTER AND JOHN YOUNG PLANETARIUM

This bright hands-on museum appeals to children and there are also exhibits on natural history. The Planetarium features weekend laser concerts.

810 E Rollins Street, Orlando (at Loch Haven). Tel: (407) 896–7151. Open: Monday to Thursday 9am–5pm, Friday 9am–9pm, Saturday noon–9pm, Sunday noon–5pm. Admission charge.

POLK MUSEUM OF ART

One of the biggest collections of pre-Columbian arts in Central Florida, with changing exhibitions of contemporary and historical art.

800 East Palmetto Street, Lakeland (50 miles SW of Orlando). Tel: (813) 688–7743. Guided tours (phone in advance). Open: Tuesday to Saturday 10am–4pm, Sunday noon–4pm. Closed Mondays, August, and holidays. Free.

REPTILE WORLD SERPENTARIUM

A rare chance to see cobras, vipers and rattlesnakes being handled by a scientific staff who also collect and distribute snake venom. The serpentarium features lizards, turtles and snakes from around the world.

5705 E Bronson Memorial Highway, St Cloud (25 miles SE of Orlando). Tel: (407) 892–6905. Open: daily 9am–5.30pm. Closed: Monday. Admission charge.

RIVER CRUISES ON THE ST JOHNS

This is a chance to see something of natural Florida. A two-hour cruise reveals hundreds of birds and fish, with alligators and bald eagles as highlights. *4359 Peninsula Point, Sanford (20 miles NE of Orlando). Open: 11am–1pm, 1.30–3.30pm (closed Monday). Tel: (407) 330–1612.*

SEA WORLD OF FLORIDA

Sea World is the most popular marine-life park in the world. The highlight is the *Shamu: New Visions* show. Staged in the 5,200-seater Shamu Stadium, it stars the Sea World killer whale family, including Baby Namu, born here in 1989. New are *Mission: Bermuda Triangle*, which mixes undersea expertise with flight simulator technology, and a children's play area. A trip up the 400-foot Sky Tower, particularly at sunset when they are testing the lasers for the evening show, gives a splendid view of the park and the whole of the Orlando area. You will need a full day to make sure you see everything that this park has to offer.
7007 Sea World Drive, Orlando. Tel: (407) 351–3600. Open: daily 9am–7pm (extended in summer).

SILVER SPRINGS

This multi-themed nature park, in its beautiful setting, has the largest artesian limestone spring in the world at its heart. Highlights are glass-bottom boat rides along the crystal waters of the Silver River and along the Lost River. In Deer Park llamas, goats and deer eat from your hand.

Adjacent is Wild Waters, a family water-playground, with a wave pool, water flumes and a racing flume.
5656 NE Florida Boulevard (SR 40), Silver Springs (75 miles northwest of Orlando). Tel: (904) 236–2121. Open: daily 9am–5pm (extended in summer). Wild Waters – open: April to May daily and September weekends 10am–5pm; June to August daily 10am–8pm.

SPLENDID CHINA

A literally splendid Chinese theme park with more than 60 miniature replicas of China's historic landmarks, from a half-mile Great Wall to the Forbidden City.

Killer whales on form at Sea World

Highway 192, in Kissimmee (12 miles SW of Orlando, 2 miles west of Disney World's main entrance road). Tel: (407) 396–7111.

UNIVERSAL STUDIOS

These are the largest working film and televison studios outside Hollywood. The format closely follows that of Disney-MGM Studios with studio tours and special-effects thrill rides based on blockbuster movie themes. Of the 40 or so rides, don't miss *Jaws*, billed as 'the explosive fury of a 28-foot, 3-ton Great White shark'. *Back to the Future* is the most advanced thrill ride that has yet been devised, and another technical masterpiece is *Kongfrontation*, in which your aerial street-car is pursued by King Kong. In *Earthquake*, you can ride a San Francisco subway train as an earthquake occurs or by way of a peaceful contrast, you can pedal above the rooftop with ET. In Nickelodeon Studios children can queue up to audition for roles in one of the popular programmes and everyone can get a behind-the-scenes look at film-making.

1000 Universal Studios Plaza (I–4 at Florida Turnpike), Orlando. Tel: (407) 363–8000. Open: from 9am, but hours vary by season. Admission charge.

WATER MANIA

Children and adults alike have fun with the slides and pools in this 38-acre park, including the Anaconda, the 72-foot Screamer and the Banana Peel. Try the Whitecaps wave pool, or the Double Berserker, test your nerve down 14 thrill slides or just picnic in the shade.

6073 W Irlo Bronson Memorial Highway, Kissimmee. Tel: (407) 396–2626. Open: March to May and September 10am–5pm; June to August 9am–9pm. Admission charge.

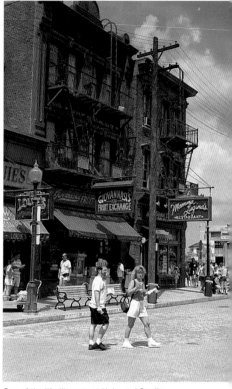

One of the life-like sets at Universal Studios

WET 'N' WILD

It really feels wet 'n' wild as you tremble on the top platform of the terrifying-looking Der Stuka, one of the world's highest speed slides, or at another of the tunnels and slides in this 25-acre park's daring array. The waves that stir the lakes are gentler, or try Knee Ski, the half-mile, cable-operated ski tow. For children under 4 feet, there are cut-down versions of the adult rides.

6200 International Drive, Orlando. Tel: (407) 351–1800. Open: daily mid-February to December. Admission charge.

BRINGING IN THE SNOWBIRDS

Every winter it seems as though Florida visitors outnumber residents. Many of these are 'snowbirds' – people from the cold Northern states, even as far as Canada, who head south to escape the frost and ice.

In Jacksonville, the main eastern gateway from the north, they pour over the border for Christmas, and on the west side, Pensacola and the snow-white beaches of the Emerald Coast are thick with sunbathers, the water crowded with surfboards and sails.

Two men, both Northerners, are largely responsible for this winter migration: Henry Flagler and Henry Plant, whose race to build the railroad down the east and west sides of Florida in turn formed the modern state. They were founders, too, of today's tourist industry, building gracious hotels which catered for the rich winter visitors. Two of these are Flagler's 1888 Ponce de León Hotel in St Augustine (now a college), and Plant's 1891 Moorish-style Tampa Hotel, part of the University of Tampa, which houses the Henry B Plant Museum.

Many of today's visitors come by car or camper van (recreation vehicle or RV) which are parked in rows alongside the beaches around Miami and other resorts, while their owners lie on the sand soaking up the sun. Others set out from Miami for a cruise in the Caribbean.

A tribute to Ponce de León, the man who discovered Florida in 1513

The Spanish-style Lightner Museum, formerly a hotel, in St Augustine

America's oldest stone fort, Castillo de San Marcos, is now a national monument and one of the chief tourist attractions in St Augustine

The Atlantic East Coast

*S*outh from Ormond Beach to Fort Lauderdale, this coast is one big beautiful beach stretching for mile after mile. Warm rollers cream in, and every community, large or small, claims that theirs is the best beach. Along this coast are some of the most famous holiday spots – Daytona Beach, Cocoa Beach and Palm Beach.

For most of its length, the coastline is screened by a long island chain, with inlets and bays which form a peaceful inland route, the Intracoastal Waterway, popular with long-distance sailors.

Millionaires, speed and space

In the 1890s, railroad magnate Henry Flagler turned Ormond Beach into the first 'Millionaires Row', on this coast. Men of fabulous wealth, such as John D Rockefeller, Henry Ford and R E Olds, lived and visited here and used the flat sands of Daytona and Ormond beaches as testing grounds for their prototype automobiles. If Daytona was to become the capital of speed, however, even more momentous happenings would be occurring a few miles further south. The National Aeronautics and Space Administration (NASA) was formed in 1958 and by the early 1960s Cape Canaveral was a by-word for space exploration.

Further south Palm Beach became the modern 'Millionaires Row' and Fort Lauderdale, a water city criss-crossed by canals, evolved into a busy commercial centre and a popular beach resort.

From Ormond Beach to New Smyrna

From Ormond Beach to Daytona Beach and beyond is a magnificent 23-mile stretch of 500-foot-wide sand. Cars are still allowed on the beach, but not to race, and today these sands are one of the state's most popular family beaches. Down at the Ponce de León Inlet, named after the Spanish adventurer, the lighthouse looks across the water to New Smyrna, founded by Minorcan settlers in the 18th century.

The Pier, unusually deserted, at Daytona

BIRTHPLACE OF SPEED MUSEUM

This disappointingly small museum, which will probably appeal only to speed aficionados, gives a brief glimpse of the days when this area was the 'Birthplace of Speed', and of the development of the automobile industry and racing. Among the few cars that are here is a replica of the record-breaking *Stanley Steamer* and a 1922 Ford Model-T.
160 East Granada Boulevard, Ormond Beach. Tel: (904) 672–5657.

*Open: Tuesday to Saturday 1pm–5pm.
Admission charge.*

THE CASEMENTS

John D Rockefeller's former winter
home, a sturdy, handsome wooden house
from 1914 to 1937, is now a cultural
centre and museum, with Rockefeller-
period rooms. The top floor features a
museum of Hungarian folk art, full of
colourful national costumes, and a boy
scout exhibit. The Rockefeller Gardens
around the house have been restored to
their original design.
*25 Riverside Drive, Ormond Beach. Tel:
(904) 676–3216. Guided tours. Open:
Monday to Thursday 9am–9pm, Friday
9am–6pm, Saturday 9am–noon.*

DAYTONA BEACH FLEA MARKET

This is one of the biggest flea markets
in Florida with hundreds of vendors
occupying 40 acres of covered and paved
areas. You can pick up anything from
citrus fruit and seafood to a penknife or
an old coin.
*Southwest corner of US 92, International
Speedway Boulevard, I–95. Tel: (904)
252–1999. Open: rain or shine, Friday to
Sunday 8am–5pm.*

DAYTONA BOARDWALK AND PIER

The Boardwalk has miniature golf, fast
food and entertainment, a bandshell for
concerts, and the Sir Malcolm Campbell
memorial. You can 'fly' over the Pier,
claimed to be the longest on America's
East Coast, on the gondola skyride, or
zoom up the Space Needle at the end of
the Pier for a panoramic view over the
heads of the many pier fishermen (see
pages 24–5).
Free. Small fishing charge.

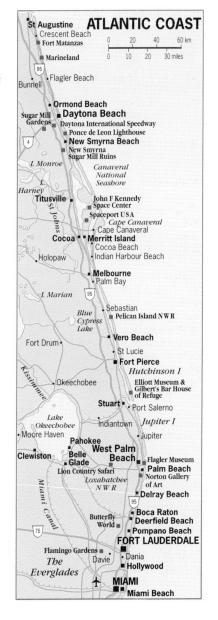

DAYTONA INTERNATIONAL SPEEDWAY

Daytona International Speedway

This mecca of speed was opened in 1959 as the World Center of Racing, staging the first Daytona 500. The '500' is the annual culmination of Speedweeks, one of the world's classic motor-sports festivals, lasting 16 days during the first half of February. Motorcycle Week in early March is the two-wheeled equivalent. It's a thrill at any time of the year, however, just to see a practice round during a guided tour.

1801 International Speedway Boulevard (US 92), Daytona Beach. Tel: (904) 254–2700. Open: 9am–5pm. Admission charge.

DAYTONA MUSEUM OF ARTS AND SCIENCES

This is the area's finest museum and features two small but outstanding art collections – Arts in America – paintings, furniture, metal, glass and needlework from 1750 to 1917; and the Cuban Collection, 200 years of Latin folk art up to 1959. The highlight for children is the unique 13-foot-high skeleton of a giant sloth found near by. There is also a Planetarium, and nature trails.

1040 Museum Boulevard, Daytona. Tel: (904) 255–0285. Open: Tuesday to Friday 9am–4pm, Saturday to Sunday noon–5pm. Admission charge (free Friday).

HALIFAX HISTORICAL MUSEUM

A small but interesting collection of historical exhibits and records relating to the local county: from a 600-year-old Indian canoe and Spanish artefacts salvaged from plantation ruins, to the early years of beach racing. The 1930s miniature of Boardwalk and Bandshell (with 1,300 tiny figures) is a favourite.

252 South Beach Street, Daytona Beach. Tel: (904) 255–6976. Guided tours. Open: Tuesday to Saturday 10am–4pm. Admission charge.

MARY McLEOD BETHUNE FOUNDATION

Eleanor Roosevelt (wife of the President) often stayed in this white frame house on the Bethune-Cookman College campus, now returned to how it was when she visited her friend, Dr Bethune.

640 Dr Mary McLeod Bethune Blvd, Daytona Beach. Tel:(904) 255–1401. Open: Monday to Friday 10am–noon, 1–4pm. Free.

NEW SMYRNA SUGAR MILL RUINS STATE HISTORIC SITE

This State Historic Site holds the best-preserved remains of one of 10 sugar mills which once stood on this coast. It was once the heart of a large plantation, managed with slave labour. The mill was attacked and burned by Seminole Indians in 1835.

West of SR 44 and south on Mission Drive, New Smyrna Beach. Tel: (904) 429–2284. Open: 8am–dusk. Admission charge.

PONCE DE LEÓN INLET LIGHTHOUSE

This 100-year-old lighthouse came out of retirement in 1982 to restart as a working lighthouse run by the Coast Guard. Make the stiff climb to the top for a view north to Daytona and over the inlet, packed with small boats, to New Smyrna Beach. Below, there are historical exhibits and a park area with picnic tables.

4931 South Peninsula Drive, Ponce Inlet. Tel: (904) 761–1821. Open: summer 10am–7pm, rest of year 10am–5pm. Admission charge.

SUGAR MILL GARDENS

The ruins of an old English sugar plantation are set in 12 acres of botanical gardens with lovely flowering trees, holly, magnolia and many other exotic plants. Children go for the 40-year-old dinosaur statues, relics of the time when the gardens were 'Bongoland'.

Herbert Street, Port Orange. Open: 8.30am–5pm. Free.

WRIGHT BROTHERS FLYER

This stylised, full-size, stainless steel replica of the Wright Flyer has electronically-powered propellers, and a full-scale diorama shows the Wright Brothers' historic flight at Kitty Hawk, North Carolina.

In front of the Jack R Hunt Memorial Library, Embry-Riddle Aeronautical University, off Clyde Morris Boulevard, south of Volusia Avenue, Daytona.

The 175-foot lighthouse at Ponce Inlet

The Space and Treasure Coasts

*F*rom the very start of the Space Age, the pioneers here were determined to stay in tune with nature, and the Space and Treasure coasts have some of the best natural areas in the east. With barrier islands, bridges, beaches and inlets, it is sometimes hard to know whether you are on mainland or island.

KENNEDY SPACE CENTER SPACEPORT USA

This is the heart of the Space Coast, where rockets blast into the sky, but somehow it still lives in harmony with the natural environment. Twenty-two species of endangered and threatened animals, fish, and birds live in the Merritt Island Wildlife Refuge alone.

There is no denying that the Kennedy Space Center is the highest of high technology, and everything is on a giant scale, from the Giant Crawler Shuttle Transporter weighing some 3,000 US tons to the 363-foot-long *Saturn V,* the largest rocket ever built in the US. You can walk round and stand

under huge machines, touch hardware displays and marvel at the size. One of the highlights of the Center is the IMAX film of a space flight that turns you into an astronaut floating above the earth. IMAX is a special, very large-scale cinema technique that takes you right into the picture as a simulator would. When this is projected on to a screen five-storeys high you actually feel as if you are there! After seeing the film take a bus tour to view some of the actual hardware. One tour shows you Apollo Mission and Space Shuttle sites, the other goes to Cape Canaveral to see the

Craft at the Kennedy Space Center

pioneer space sites. Back at the Galaxy Center there is the Gallery of Space Flight to visit, more films to see and the famous 'rocket park' where numerous historic craft point proudly skywards.
John F Kennedy Space Center, NASA Parkway (SR 405), Merritt Island. Tel: (407) 452–2121. Open: 9am–dusk. Closed: Christmas Day. Admission to Spaceport USA free, charge for tours and IMAX. Allow 5 to 6 hours.

ASTRONAUT MEMORIAL PLANETARIUM AND OBSERVATORY
There is a small museum here including a model of John Glenn's space capsule, but the big attraction is the planetarium where you can explore the universe through Florida's largest telescope. Laser shows on Friday and Saturday nights.
Brevard Community College, 1519 Clearlake Road, Cocoa. Tel: (407) 632–1111. Guided tours. Free. Planetarium charge.

BREVARD ART CENTER AND MUSEUM
This large, attractive, modern facility is renowned for the quality of its touring art exhibitions from major collections and contemporary artists.
1463 North Highland Avenue, Melbourne. Tel: (407) 242–0737. Guided tours. Open: Tuesday to Saturday 10am–4pm, Sunday noon–4pm. Admission charge.

BREVARD MUSEUM OF HISTORY AND NATURAL SCIENCE
Children love the Discovery Room, adults enjoy the turn-of-the-century kitchen, and there are many other intriguing reminders of the area's past. There is a natural science area plus 22 acres of nature trails.

The Astronaut Hall of Fame

2201 Michigan Avenue, Cocoa. Tel: (407) 632–1830. Guided tours. Open: Tuesday to Saturday 10am–4pm, Sunday 1pm–4pm. Admission charge.

ELLIOTT MUSEUM
Allow at least a couple of hours for the different wings of this large, eclectic museum. If you are short of time, concentrate on the Americana from 1865 onwards with 14 reconstructed shops, and a real Indian chickee dwelling. See also the '1914 Garage' with an outstanding collection of vintage automobiles.
825 NE Ocean Boulevard, Stuart. Tel: (407) 225–1961 for opening times. Admission charge.

ENERGY ENCOUNTER
This is designed as a journey through the world of energy, with the mysteries of electricity and nuclear power explained by various exhibits.
Northern entrance of St Lucie Nuclear Power Plant on A1A, Hutchinson Island. Tel: (407) 468–4111. Open: Tuesday to Friday and Sunday 10am–4pm.

FORT PIERCE INLET STATE RECREATION AREA

A 340-acre park of Atlantic beach, dunes and coastal hammock, with Jack Island, on the Intracoastal Waterway, a bird-watcher's paradise. Swimming, some of the Treasure Coasts' safest surfing, picnic areas and hiking and nature trails are all on offer.

2200 Atlantic Beach Boulevard, Fort Pierce (four miles east of Fort Pierce, via north Causeway to Atlantic Beach Boulevard). Tel: (407) 468–3985. Admission and camping charge.

A heron resting at Merritt Island. The refuge has three walking trails

GILBERT'S BAR HOUSE OF REFUGE

This is the only survivor of nine refuge houses commissioned in 1875 by the US Lifesaving Service. Refuge houses provided food and shelter to survivors of shipwrecks. It was still in Coast Guard use in World Wars I and II, and now functions as a maritime museum and small aquarium.

301 MacArthur Boulevard, Hutchinson Island. Tel: (407) 225–1875. Tours. Open: Tuesday to Sunday 1–4pm. Admission charge.

LITTLE RIVER QUEEN

Dine and dance as the sun sets on this charming paddleboat, which cruises along the Banana River from Gatsby's Dockside.

480 Cocoa Beach Causeway. Tel: (407) 783–2380. Open: daily 2pm, weeknights 6.30pm, Friday to Saturday 7pm.

MERRITT ISLAND NATIONAL WILDLIFE REFUGE

Adjacent to the Space Center, this wildlife refuge is a habitat for wintering migratory waterfowl and has more than 310 species of birds, 25 mammals, 117 types of fish and 65 different amphibians and reptiles. Of these, sadly 22 are endangered or threatened species.

Reached by Highway 406. Tel: (407) 867–0667. Visitor centre open: Monday to Friday 8am–4.30pm, weekends 9am–7pm.

OLD COCOA VILLAGE

An historic collection of 50 shops and eating places cluster round oak-shaded pavements and cobbled streets. The Porcher House, built in 1916 and once home to the county's largest citrus grower, is open to the public. The old

Vaudeville Theatre still stages live shows and children's theatre.
Cocoa. Tel: (407) 636–5050 for information/tickets. Brevard Museum offers twice-weekly village walking tours. Ask at the Porcher House.

ST LUCIE COUNTY HISTORICAL MUSEUM

Here you can see artefacts relating to Spanish shipwrecks and Seminole Indians and a guide will take you around the adjacent 1907 Gardener House with furnishings from the 1880s to the 1920s. Among the exhibits is a collection of local late-19th-century photographs.
414 Seaway Drive, Fort Pierce. Tel: (407) 468–1795. Open: Tuesday to Saturday 10am–4pm, Sunday noon– 4pm. Admission charge.

SPACE COAST SCIENCE CENTER

If you have ever wondered what a dinosaur egg feels like, how freeze-dried astronaut food tastes or what a 'million' really looks like, then this small, friendly hands -on Discovery Center will enlighten you!
1500 Highland Avenue, Melbourne. Tel:
(407) 259–5572. Open: Tuesday to Friday 10am–5pm, Saturday 10am–4pm.

SPESSARD HOLLAND PARK AND PLAYALINDA BEACH

Watching turtles is fascinating and the Space Coast has them galore. These are among the largest American turtle-nesting beaches. Loggerheads, greens, leatherbacks – all protected under the Endangered Species Act – come ashore to lay their eggs during the May to September nesting season.
Spessard Holland Park. Tel: (407) 676–1701 for information and directions. Playalinda. Tel: (407) 867–2805.

VALIANT AIR COMMAND MUSEUM

An outstanding collection of 350 military aircraft, including artefacts and exhibits from both World Wars and Desert Storm. Flying displays are held in March.
6600 Tico Road, Titusville. Tel: (407) 268–1941. Admission charge.

A P-51 Mustang on show at the Valiant Air Command Museum

LIFE'S A BEACH

You're probably either an east or a west coaster; you may like your beaches bold and brassy – all waverunners and waterskiers – or completely natural, just water and wildlife. But, whatever the beach, Florida has it somewhere.

In the west, the Pinellas and the Lee Island Coast, and many other places, celebrate the sunset. On the hotel decks, jutting out over the beach, bar staff make up the sundowners and there's a sudden silence, then the toast, as the last curve of the crimson disc disappears below reds, yellows and oranges painted on to the sea.

In the east, on stretches such as Miami Beach, the most famous beach in the state, you wait for sun up on early mornings which already feel

warm. Slowly the sky lightens until that living moment when the sun appears and it's time for a dip in the Atlantic. This 10-mile stretch has areas to suit all tastes, from quiet, lazy nooks to lively, bare-as-much-as-you-dare spots.

For something even more brash and bouncy, try Daytona Beach, 23 miles from New Smyrna to Ormond Beach. It is at its most lively at spring break when thousands of college revellers descend on it in search of a good time. The beach has, of course, always been synonymous with the motor car. Here, in 1935, Sir Malcolm Campbell covered the firm white sand at the astonishing, record-breaking speed of 276mph. He was part of a tradition of speed which started in

For the more energetic, watersports of all kinds are on offer at Key West

Daytona and lasts today – you can drive along the beach, though the speed limit is now a decorous 10mph!

For peace, quiet and a natural setting, try the Cape Canaveral National Seashore and Treasure Island Coast, particularly near Spaceport USA, which shares a boundary with Merritt Island National Wildlife Refuge.

Last of all, for a beach that sums up Florida, drive almost to Key West for continental America's southernmost sands, Bahia Honda, a peaceful tree-lined paradise, where you can swim in the morning in the Atlantic Ocean, and dip into the Gulf of Mexico after lunch.

Lively and modern, the resort of Fort Lauderdale has beaches to rival Miami's

Hundreds of varieties of beautiful shells add to the pleasure of time spent on the beach at Sanibel Island

More sun, sand and palms at Key West

In and Around Palm Beach

*P*alm Beach is polo, Rolls-Royces and jewellery shops with million-dollar price tickets. The towering, luxuriant palms that are such a feature here owe their life to a Spanish brig, shipwrecked on its way to Cadiz. When its cargo of coconuts washed ashore, the settlers decided to plant them. You cannot miss the result today.

ANN NORTON SCULPTURE GARDENS

This is where Ann Weaver Norton, wife of Ralph Norton, who founded the Norton Gallery, had her studio. You can find her monumental sculptures hidden among lavish tropical gardens which contain one of the most notable palm collections in Florida.

Barcelona Road, West Palm Beach. Tel: (407) 832–5328. Open: Tuesday to Saturday noon–4pm. Admission charge.

DREHER PARK ZOO

More than 400 animals, including 100 native species, live in this 25-acre zoo; the tiny Florida marmoset and the rare Florida panther are among them. There is a petting zoo for children.

1301 Summit Boulevard, West Palm Beach. Tel: (407) 547–WILD. Guided tours (in advance). Open: 9am–5pm year-round. Admission charge.

HENRY MORRISON FLAGLER MUSEUM

Whitehall Mansion, the home of the man who founded Palm Beach as a playground of the rich, was once called 'more wonderful than any palace in Europe'. Completed in 1902 at a cost of $4 million, its palatial great halls, music room, billiard room, library, dining rooms and bedrooms are decorated in historic European styles and give an idea of the opulent lifestyle enjoyed in that era by Flagler and his illustrious guests. Don't miss the ornate ceilings and his private railway car.

Just south of Royal Poinciana Plaza on Coconut Row, Palm Beach. Tel: (407) 655–2833. Guided tours (in advance). Open: Tuesday to Saturday 10am–5pm, Sunday noon–5pm. Closed: Mondays, Christmas and New Year.

JUPITER LIGHTHOUSE

This red brick tower, built in 1860 to warn ships of the dangerous shoals lying off shore, is the oldest building in Palm Beach County. It played a part in the Civil War and right up to World War II. You can learn more about this prosperous community at the neighbouring Loxahatchee Historical Society Museum.

At junction of Loxahatchee river and Intracoastal Waterway, Jupiter. Tel: (407) 747–6639. Open: Sundays.

LION COUNTRY SAFARI

You may well find the long neck of a giraffe bending to your car as you drive among hundreds of wild animals in Florida's only self-drive safari. A Safari World boat cruise, a petting zoo and an amusement park complete a good half-day's excursion.

Southern Boulevard West (SR 80). Tel: (407) 793–1084. Guided tours.

Open: 9.30am–5.30pm year round. Admission charge.

Norton Gallery of Art, West Palm Beach

LOXAHATCHEE NATIONAL WILDLIFE REFUGE

This beautiful wilderness area, covering 221 square miles of unspoiled Everglades, is an ideal day out. See it from an airboat or rent your own motorboat or canoe. Anglers can enjoy some of the finest bigmouth bass fishing in the country; birdwatchers should look out for the rare snail kite, rails, limpkins and herons.

14900 Lox Road West, West Palm Beach. Tel: (407) 734–8303. Open: 30 minutes before dawn to 30 minutes after dusk. Admission charge.

NORTON GALLERY OF ART

This is one of the best collections of Impressionist and Post-Impressionist works of art in Florida, held in this very highly acclaimed small gallery. There is also a priceless Chinese jade collection and outstanding sculpture by Moore, Picasso and Dégas.

1451 S Olive Avenue, West Palm Beach. Tel: (407) 832–5194. Guided tours. Open: Tuesday to Saturday 10am–5pm, Sunday 1–5pm. Donations accepted.

SOUTH FLORIDA SCIENCE MUSEUM

The hands-on science exhibits here absorb children and adults alike. There is also a planetarium and aquarium.

4801 Dreher Trail N, West Palm Beach. Tel: (407) 832–1988. Guided tours. Open: 9.30am–5pm daily; Friday also: 6.30–10pm. Admission charge.

STAR OF PALM BEACH

Get a glimpse from the water of the ritzy lifestyle of the super-rich, with views into the grounds of the mansions of the famous. Sightseeing, luncheon and dinner cruises on a 300-passenger replica Hudson River steamer.

900 E Blue Heron Boulevard, Singer Island. Tel: (407) 842–0882. Phone for times and luncheon/dinner reservations.

THE BREAKERS

Have at least a drink or a coffee in this glorious old hotel right on the Atlantic. Built in 1926 by Henry Flagler in Italian Renaissance style, it echoes with the elegance of a bygone era.

1 S County Road, Palm Beach. Tel: (407) 655–6611.

Greater Fort Lauderdale

*F*ort Lauderdale has often been called the 'Venice of the Americas' and 300 miles of navigable inland waterways reinforce its nickname. Though the 'gondoliers' may not sing Italian songs, water taxis are popular. The Intracoastal Waterway flows through the heart of the city and most of the city's important buildings lie close to the water. With Port Everglades the second largest cruise port in Florida and 23 miles of beach along an azure sea, the emphasis in Fort Lauderdale and its neighbouring communities is firmly on the waterfront.

ART AND CULTURE CENTER OF HOLLYWOOD

This centre presents performing and visual arts right beside the ocean. In addition there are changing cultural, historical and art exhibitions, with jazz and classical concerts.

1301 S Ocean Drive, Hollywood. Tel: (305) 921–3274. Open: Tuesday to Saturday 10am–4pm, Sunday 1–4pm, Thursday 7–10pm. Admission charge.

Get in touch at the imaginative and innovative hands-on Discovery Center

ATLANTIS THE WATER KINGDOM

South Florida's largest water theme park comprises 65 acres of slides, rides, shows and attractions. Pluck up courage and try the hair-raising Awesome Two-Some, a thrilling tandem tube ride, and dozens more rides.

2700 Stirling Road, Hollywood. Tel: (305) 926–1001. Open: April to June 10am–5pm, late June to August 10am–10pm. Closed: end October to March. Admission charge.

BONNET HOUSE

This grand 1920s, Florida-style plantation home and estate was the winter home of the well-known American artist and collector, Frederick Clay Bartlett. Sitting in 35 splendid acres, its 30 beautiful rooms contain a treasure trove of fine decorative art (see page 33).

900 N Birch Road, Fort Lauderdale. Tel: (305) 563–5393. Guided tours by reservation May to November, Tuesday and Thursday 10am and 1.30pm, Sunday 1.30pm. Admission charge.

BUTTERFLY WORLD

Walk through lush tropical gardens among a flutter of thousands of exotic butterflies. Exhibits include butterfly

breeding, an insectarium and a water garden.
Tradewinds Park, 3600 W Sample Road, Coconut Creek. Tel: (305) 977–4400. Guided tours, phone in advance. Open: Monday to Saturday 9am–5pm, Sunday 1–5pm. Admission charge.

DISCOVERY CENTER
A diverse and ingenious hands-on science, art and history museum for all the family. Touch a star or rummage around in the Florida Finds Room (see page 33).
401 SW 2nd Avenue, Fort Lauderdale. Tel: (305) 467–6637. Guided tours. Open: Monday to Saturday 10am–5pm, Sunday noon–5pm. Admission charge.

EVERGLADES HOLIDAY PARK AIRBOAT TOURS
An exciting way to see the natural world of the Everglades.
21940 Griffin Road, Fort Lauderdale. Tel: (305) 434–8111. Tours: 9am–5pm daily. Charge.

FLAMINGO GARDENS
These colourful gardens, full of exotic and native plants in an Everglades setting, are home to a large flock of brilliant pink flamingos. Take a tram tour, see the Everglades Museum and the Crocodile Lagoon.
3750 Flamingo Road, Davie. Tel: (305) 473-2955. Tours: 9am–5pm. Admission charge.

OCEAN WORLD
The star turn at this small marine-life park is the excellent dolphin and sea-lion show. You can also watch sharks feeding, see an exotic bird show and touch and feed the dolphins (see page 33).

Step aboard the *Jungle Queen* which offers three-hour cruises along New River, taking in the sights of Fort Lauderdale

1701 SE 17th Street, Fort Lauderdale. Tel: (305) 525–6611. Open: 10am–6pm. Admission charge.

VOYAGER SIGHTSEEING TRAM
The best introduction to Fort Lauderdale is a Voyager Tram tour: a lively, informative, 90-minute tour takes in all the main sights, past palm-lined streets, fishing fleets and yacht basins.
600 Seabreeze Boulevard, Fort Lauderdale. Tel: (305) 463–0401. Tours: 8.45am–4pm. Admission charge.

In and Around Greater Miami

*T*his is a city of the future, with tall, shiny buildings spiking up towards the sky, interspersed with early architecture. The streets hold a babble of voices in many languages, as North Americans, Caribbeans, Cubans, South Americans, and Europeans jostle in a mixture of shapes, colours and cultures.

Orange blossom birth

Miami owes its birth to the late-19th-century socialite Julia Tuttle. Her dream was to tame this tangled jungle and to bring people in. Legend has it she intrigued the railroad baron, Henry Flagler, by sending fresh orange blossom to show that the area had escaped the Great 1894–5 Frost. Flagler recognised the tourism potential of such a mild climate, extended his railroad south and thus founded modern Miami.

Miami is an exciting city, noisy, busy, even dangerous in some areas. Its bridges arch across the blue-green water, streaked white with sails and the wakes of motor boats. Odd as it may seem, in the land of the automobile, Miami and Fort Lauderdale have retained a sense of historical priorities and give a ship right of way when it comes to a drawbridge.

Diverse communities

This sprawling metropolis stretches down as far as Homestead and Florida City, some 25 miles south, and north towards Fort Lauderdale, with districts that are distinct communities in their own right. There are a multitude of islands, linked by bridges, Miami Beach with its 1920s Art Deco architecture, and the beautiful sub-tropical beach retreat of Key Biscayne. Below the causeway to the mainland, the sea is a windsurfer's paradise. South of here the small keys below Key Biscayne form the Biscayne National Park.

Just north of Miami Beach, on the long narrow island that skirts the bay, tiny communities reach as far as Sunny Isles Beach. Bal Harbour is the resort of the rich, with elegant condominiums and the famous Bal Harbour Shopping Center.

Some mainland districts feature flights-of-fancy by 1920s developers – Arabian-style designs in Opa-Locka, and Mediterranean-style villages in Coral Gables. Little Havana feels like a miniature of the Cuban capital, pre-Castro. Homestead is the gateway to both the Everglades and Biscayne Bay national parks. Coconut Grove is one of the oldest communities in Miami, a gathering of artists, intellectuals and old Miami families in an area of narrow red-brick pavements and Victorian street lamps.

Little Haiti captures the sights, smells and sounds of the Caribbean, with a colourful marketplace and every sort of Caribbean craft. Once known as Lemon City, this is now the heart of the Haitian community and is the best place to try old Caribbean specialities such as *tassot* (fried goat) and *griot* (fried pork).

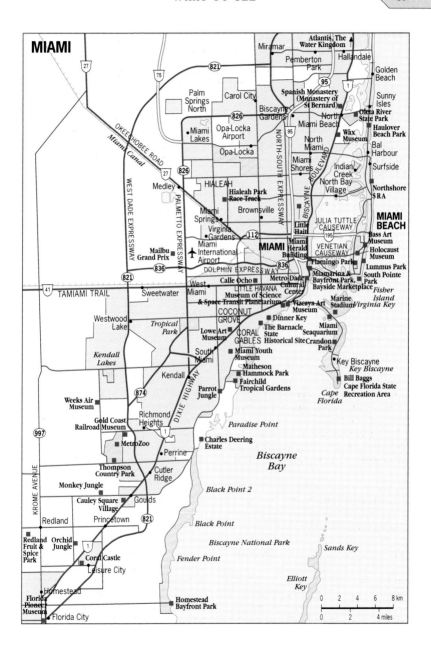

SEEING THE SIGHTS

The best way to get a snapshot view of Miami is to take an Old Town Trolley Tour. This circular, 90-minute guided tour leaves every half hour from Bayside Marketplace, with stops at the Miami Seaquarium, Vizcaya, Museum of Science and Space Transit Planetarium, Coconut Grove and Coral Gables. Another circuit tours Miami Beach (tours every two hours). You can hop on and off where you like.
Old Town Trolley, Bayside Marketplace. Tel: (305) 374–8687. Tours: City Tour 10am–4pm daily; Miami Beach Tour 10.45am–4.45pm.

See the sights of Miami from a trolley

AMERICAN POLICE HALL OF FAME AND MUSEUM

An overwhelming 10,000 items in this museum range from firearms to an electric chair, a prison cell, and a St Valentine's Day Massacre scene. A huge marble memorial honours the 3,000-plus US police officers who have been killed on duty since 1960.
3801 Biscayne Boulevard. Tel: (305) 573–0070. Guided tours. Open: 10am–5.30pm daily. Admission charge.

THE BARNACLE

One of Coconut Grove's earliest settlers, Commodore Ralph Middleton Munroe, did much to preserve the so-called 'Era of the Bay', and designed this unusual pioneer home in 1891.
3485 Main Highway, Coconut Grove. Tel: (305) 448–9445. Open: 9am–4pm daily. Admission charge.

BAYFRONT PARK

Next to Bayside Marketplace along Biscayne Bay, the park offers a cool shelter against the midday sun, with a fine view of the boats. Don't miss tributes to famous people, notably the John F Kennedy Memorial Torch of Friendship with its eternal flame.
100 Biscayne Boulevard, off Brickell Road.

BAYSIDE MARKETPLACE

The hub of central Miami, right on Biscayne Bay marina, this bustling complex of shops, eating places and buskers is the perfect place to soak up the vibrant multi-ethnic Miami scene. Enjoy a Cuban coffee, watch the Brazilian samba competition or take a gondola trip around the bay.
401 Biscayne Boulevard. Tel: (305) 577–3344. Open: Monday to Saturday 10am–10pm, Sunday: noon–8pm.

BILL BAGGS CAPE FLORIDA STATE RECREATION AREA

This superb mile-long beach enjoys a picturesque pine grove setting, with the 1825 Cape Florida Lighthouse at its far end. Take your own food along and enjoy a picnic or barbecue in the specially provided areas.

Via Rickenbacker Causeway, to Key Biscayne. Tel: (305) 361–5811. Open: 8am–sunset. Admission charge.

CAULEY SQUARE VILLAGE

This 10-acre historic railroad village, converted into a shopping area, gives a stylised insight into south Florida's early pioneer life.

22400 Old Dixie Highway (north of Homestead). Tel: (305) 258–3543. Guided tours. Open: Monday to Saturday 10am–4.30pm. Free.

CORAL CASTLE

A unique and mind-boggling achievement of 1,000 US tons of coral sculptures and buildings, with furniture to match, created singlehandedly by Ed Leedskalnin, a Latvian immigrant, between 1920 and 1940. How did he do it, why did he do it? You may find the answers here.

28655 S Dixie Highway, Homestead. Tel: (305) 248–6344. Guided tours. Open: 9am–9pm daily. Admission charge.

CORAL GABLES MERRICK HOUSE

This was the boyhood home of George E Merrick, who founded the city of Coral Gables. The original 1898 wooden structure had a two-storey extension made from local coral.

907 Coral Way, Coral Gables. Tel: (305) 460–5361. Open: Sunday and Wednesday only, 1–4pm. Admission charge.

Coral Gables, home of George E Merrick

EVERGLADES ALLIGATOR FARM

Explore the vast richness of the state's flora and fauna at one of Southern Florida's oldest alligator farms. There are daily reptile shows and exhibits.

40351 SW 192nd Avenue, Homestead. Tel: (305) AIR–BOAT. Open: 9am–6pm daily. Admission charge.

FAIRCHILD TROPICAL GARDEN

The garden and lakes here are home to some 5,000 different plants in America's largest tropical botanical garden.

10901 Old Cutler Road, Coral Gables. Tel: (305) 667–1651. Open: 9.30am–4.30pm daily. Admission charge.

LITTLE HAVANA

In the 1960s, the first sight of the United States for the thousands of Cuban refugees fleeing Castro's regime, was the tall Spanish Mediterranean-style tower, built in 1925, down by the harbour. It became the Cuban refugee-processing centre and took on the name the Freedom Tower.

Most of those early refugees settled around SW 8th Street, or 'Calle Ocho' in the vernacular. The area came to be known as Little Havana, and is still the heart of the Cuban community.

Here old men in *guyaberas* sit at pavement cafés oblivious of everything but their dominoes. From the doorways floats the smell of exotic cooking – spices, paella, fried plantains, strong coffee and the tang of rich Cuban cigars –

while Latin rhythms pulsate along the streets.

There are small ethnic shops and stalls selling exotic fruits and vegetables all along Little Havana, and the Cubans still hand-roll their famous cigars in the area's small cigar factories.

Both locals and visitors pour into the eating houses and nightspots of Little Havana. Cuban dishes are simple yet exotic, and the nightclubs are loud with the sound of hip-swinging salsa music.

The highlight of the year is the Carnaval in March. Around a million people take to the streets over nine festive days, turning Calle Ocho into one huge street party.

Little Havana's Calle Ocho

Calle Ocho's Carnaval – one huge street party

Havana cigars are considered the best in the world

FRUIT AND SPICE PARK

Over 200 species and 500 varieties of
fruits, nuts and spices from all around
the world grow in this 20-acre park.
Helpful hints on vegetable and herb
garden cultivation are given and fruit
and spices are on sale.

*24801 SW 187th Avenue, Homestead (20
miles south). Tel: (305) 247–5727. Guided
tours by request. Open: 10am–5pm daily.*

GOLD COAST RAILROAD MUSEUM

For rail buffs, this ramshackle,
atmospheric, outdoor museum collection
of old steam locomotives and rolling
stock includes carriages used by US
Presidents. Go at the weekend when a
1913 train gets up steam for rides.

*12450 SW 152nd Street (near Metrozoo),
Kendall. Tel: (305) 253–7834. Guided
tours. Open: weekdays 11.30am–4.30pm,
weekends 10am–5pm. Admission charge.*

METRO-DADE CULTURAL CENTER AND HISTORICAL MUSEUM OF SOUTHERN FLORIDA

This modern block is home to the
Center for Fine Arts and the Historical
Museum of Southern Florida. The
former is dedicated to large-scale art
exhibitions. Dip into Florida's past at the
historical museum by experiencing its
jungle atmosphere of 10,000 years ago.
Explore a section of a life-size Spanish
fort, while closer to the present is a
fascinating collection of early railroad
memorabilia, old streetcars, turn-of-
the-century postcards and sepia
photographs.

*101 W Flagler Street, Miami. Tel: (305)
375–1492. Open: Monday to Saturday
10am–5pm (Thursday 9pm), Sunday
noon–5pm. Admission charge.*

Miami Seaquarium, where there are daily
shows to entertain the family

MIAMI METROZOO

Miami MetroZoo is hailed as the finest
zoo in Florida with a near-natural,
largely cage-free environment, where
only a few feet of moat separates you
from the animals. The stars are the
majestic rare white Bengal tigers and the
lovable koalas. With its outstanding
walk-through tropical aviary, some 2,800
animals and a variety of shows, this is a
great family day out. A two-mile
monorail circuit, giving a splendid
bird's-eye view, spans the four different
'continents' and aviary, with stops along
the way.

*12400 SW 152nd Street, Kendall (South
Miami). Tel: (305) 251–0400. Guided
tours. Open: 9.30am–5.30pm daily.
Admission charge.*

MIAMI NICE EXCURSIONS

Leave the car behind and go sightseeing
with one of Miami's longest-established
tour operators. Choose from tours such
as Miami at Night, Miami by Sailboat or
a motorboat ride along the Intracoastal
Waterway. Day and longer visits are
available to the Everglades, and further.
Charge varies.

*16100 Collins Avenue, Suite 104, Miami
Beach. Tel: (305) 949–9180.*

MIAMI SEAQUARIUM

Founded in 1955, Seaquarium is South Florida's largest and best marine-life exhibition. There's Lolita, the 10,000-pound Killer Whale, a shark channel, aquaria galore, a touch pool and a breeding manatee colony. The shows in the 2,500-seat stadium are exemplary, combining a little gentle education, polished performances and an abundance of good humour. Allow a full half-day to take in all the shows. There is also a gift shop and refreshment stops, and baby strollers are available.
4400 Rickenbacker Causeway. Tel: (305) 361–5705. Open: from 9.30am (closing time varies by season). Admission charge.

MICCOSUKEE INDIAN VILLAGE AND AIRBOAT TOURS

Miccosukee Indians mix tourism and their old way of life in the Everglades, guiding tours, demonstrating traditional crafts and cookery, wrestling alligators, and telling folklore tales. The museum has films and artefacts from many tribes. An airboat ride takes you deep into the Everglades, and to a 100-year-old Indian camp. There is also a restaurant serving Miccosukee specialities and a shop selling native handicrafts.
West 30 miles on Tamiami Trail. Mile Marker 70, Highway 41. Tel: (305) 223–8380 Monday to Friday; (305) 223–8388 Saturday and Sunday. Open: daily 9am–5pm. Admission charge.

MONKEY JUNGLE

Monkey Jungle has been welcoming visitors for over 50 years, ever since animal behaviourist Joseph DuMond released six Java monkeys into a dense Florida tropical hardwood hammock. Today, visitors are caged in safe protective walkways and the monkeys roam free. There is a wild monkey swimming pool and an ape encounter in a rainforest, where creatures roam in their natural element.
14805 SW 216 Street, near Homestead. Tel: (305) 235–1611. Open: 9.30am–5pm year-round. Admission charge.

Moonlight and neon brighten Miami Bayside

MUSEUM OF SCIENCE AND SPACE TRANSIT PLANETARIUM

Explore the mysteries of light and space with more than 150 hands-on exhibitions and live demonstrations. The planetarium gives multi-media and laser shows. (Call (305) 854–2222 for times and free observatory sessions.) Watch giant insects and reptiles in the Animal Exploratorium.

3280 South Miami Avenue. Tel: (305) 854–4247. Open: 10am–6pm. Admission charge.

Brilliant plumage at Parrot Jungle, one of Miami's oldest attractions

PARROT JUNGLE AND GARDENS

Wander through a natural sub-tropical garden and jungle and enjoy the sights of some 1,200 exotic birds. Most are caged, but some fly freely. Specially trained birds give six shows per day and there is a baby bird training area. Flamingo Lake has 75 brilliant pink Caribbean flamingos.

11000 SW 57th Avenue, South Miami. Tel: (305) 666–7834. Guided tours (in advance). Open: 9.30am–6pm year-round. Admission charge.

THE SPANISH MONASTERY

The oldest building in the western hemisphere, this 12th-century Spanish monastery was brought from Segovia to America in the 1960s by publisher William Randolph Hearst.

16711 W Dixie Highway, N Miami Beach. Tel: (305) 945–1461. Open: Monday to Saturday 10am–4pm, Sunday noon–5pm. Closed: Monday.

UNIVERSITY OF MIAMI – LOWE ART MUSEUM

Many changing exhibitions from its own collection. Permanent collection: Kress Collection of Renaissance and Baroque Art and Cintas Foundation of Spanish Masterpieces. Also 19th- and 20th-century American, and Native American art. Guided tours and facilities for disabled people.

1301 Stanford Drive, Coral Gables. Tel: (305) 284–3636. Open: Tuesday to Saturday 10am–5pm, Sunday noon–5pm. Closed: Monday.

THE VENETIAN POOL

Right in the heart of Coral Gables, this lovely pool was carved out of coral rock, with caves, stone bridges and a sandy beach. The water is a constant 75°F. Once, famous swimmers such as Johnny

Architectural detail at Vizcaya

Weissmuller gave exhibitions here and the Venetian Pool still has similar events today. But the real charm is to swim in such beautiful surroundings.
2701 DeSoto Boulevard, Coral Gables. Tel: (305) 460–5356. Open: Monday to Friday 11am–7.30pm, Saturday and Sunday 10am–4.30pm. Admission charge.

VIZCAYA MUSEUM AND GARDENS

This astonishingly authentic copy of a Renaissance villa was built in 1916 by the industrialist James Deering as a winter retreat, and furnished with priceless European antiques. The house is grouped round an inner courtyard where this lonely bachelor entertained under the open skies (now covered for protection). The front entrance, once also open to the sea, faces the superb gardens and the sweep of Biscayne Bay. A quarter of a million people arrive each year, but in 1987 two special visitors had a private meeting here – Pope John Paul II and President Ronald Reagan.
3251 South Miami Avenue, Coconut Grove. Tel: (305) 579–2708. Guided tours. Open: 9.30am–5pm. Admission charge.

CRUISE CAPITAL OF THE WORLD

The best place to see the great ships steaming in and out of Miami is from South Pointe at the southern tip of Miami Beach, or from a hotel window along Ocean Boulevard at sunrise where Spanish treasure galleons once sailed past on their way to and from Havana. The huge dark shapes that now flow across the horizon carry holidaymakers to and from the Caribbean.

Miami is the cruise capital of the world, home port to 19 ships from some 10 different cruise lines with a yearly total of over 3 million passengers. Always, the ships get bigger. Royal Caribbean's *Sovereign* and *Majesty of the Seas* are as tall as the Statue of Liberty. In 1993, Carnival Cruise Lines added its newest ship, the *Sensation* with 2,600 passengers. A new trend is the *American Adventure*, which carries 1,500 passengers, for families only.

At the beginning of this century, big ships were unable to reach Miami because the waterways were too shallow. It was that indefatigable railroad builder, Henry Flagler, who came to the rescue, by dredging a 12-foot canal. However, when he wanted to bring his own SS *Miami* into its home port, he realised it had a 16-foot draught! The US Army came to his rescue by dredging out what later became Government Cut, to a depth of 18 feet.

The main cruise destination out of Miami is a week lazing in the Caribbean with every conceivable amenity and entertainment on board, but there are also shorter cruises to the Bahamas, and popular round trips which simply give a taste of a life of luxury on the ocean without going anywhere.

Miami does not have it all its own way. To the north is Port Everglades, with 10 cruise lines, and glittering Palm Beach, Port Canaveral and St Petersburg are all important cruise terminals in their own right.

The *Nieuw Amsterdam* alongside the harbour at Key West

ntic cruise liners docked
e port of Miami

A smaller but no less luxurious
vessel off the Pinellas Suncoast

Miami Beach

*A*round a century ago, Miami Beach was little more than a sandy key, where fruit grower John Collins struggled to raise avocados. It was not until Henry Flagler's railroad pulled into town that the development of 'America's sun porch' really began.

The combination of a luxurious sub-tropical retreat and frontier opportunities lured tycoons, who in turn sought to attract tourists by creating a fantasy land where they could forget their cold northern climes and the Great Depression.

First heyday

In the 1920s and 1930s, Miami Beach took off. The style that came to epitomise this brave new resort was Art Deco. Every new Miami Beach Hotel was designed with futuristic streamlined shaping, neon strip lighting, cool terrazzo marble interiors and bright pastel exteriors.

The Great Depression of 1929, the South Florida building boom of the late 1930s, then the onset of war sent Miami Beach in and out of fashion for decades. By the late 1970s it had become neglected and run-down. However, in 1979 the city finally realised that its unique Art Deco architecture was its saving grace – the best possible symbol of a resort that was modern with a touch of old-fashioned style, and 'All American' yet distinctly tropical. The

The confectionary colours and pastel shades of Art Deco

Art Deco District was listed as the only 20th-century district on the National Register of Historic Places and millions of dollars were pumped into its restoration.

Colourful buildings, vibrant life

Today, SoBe, as South Miami Beach is known, is enjoying a second hey-day, with the striking pastels of Art Deco at the heart of the district. Even the beach has been restored along with bordering Lummus Park. A little further north is a new boardwalk where thousands of holidaymakers stroll to take the sea air each day. On the landward side, the old hotels have regained their former glory and a whole new generation of restaurants, shops and art centres has sprung up.

When Michael Mann set the television programme *Miami Vice* here, it proved the old adage that no publicity is bad publicity. Miami Beach was discovered by fashion photographers and that, in turn, brought in the film-makers.

Deeper hues on an Art Deco hotel

Today Miami Beach and its Art Deco hotels are known all over the world..

ART DECO DISTRICT WALKING TOURS

The Miami Design Preservation League offers Saturday tours, guided by experts, and these leisurely strolls are the best introduction to the finer points. (See also the walk on pages 30–1.)
Miami Design Preservation League, 1001 Ocean Drive, Miami Beach. Tel: (305) 672-2014. Guidebooks also available here.

ART DECO DISTRICT BICYCLE TOURS

This is a guided family cycle tour of the District on Sundays. Children's bikes and baby seats are available.
Cycles on the Beach, 14/21 Washington Avenue. Tel: (305) 673-2055 for information and reservations. Tours: 10am–6pm daily.

BASS MUSEUM OF ART

This Art Deco building, built by Russell Pancoast, grandson of Miami Beach pioneer John Collins, and now on the National Register of Historic Places, is the cultural centrepiece of Miami Beach. Its collection ranges from Rubens, Rembrandt and Toulouse-Lautrec to modern American painters like Roy Lichtenstein. There are films, concerts, exhibitions, and an innovative shop.
2121 Park Avenue. Tel: (305) 673–7533. Open: Tuesday to Saturday 10am–5pm, Sunday 1–5pm. Admission charge.

HOLOCAUST MEMORIAL

This is a very moving memorial, erected in 1990 and inspired by a small group of Miami Holocaust survivors. A huge bronze arm and hand, its wrist tattooed

Take the Old Town Trolley Tour to Miami Beach

with a number, is flung skyward making a striking first impact. On entering the museum you pass a black marble wall etched with photographs of tragic Holocaust events. A tunnel leads to an inner courtyard built of Jerusalem marble around the great arm, with stark, naked figures struggling up it. More figures on the marble floor form striking vignettes. The way out is lined with hundreds of thousands of names, a memorial to those who died (see page 31).
Meridian Avenue and Dale Boulevard. Information – Holocaust Memorial Committee, tel: (305) 538–1663. Open: 9am–9pm daily. Free, donations welcome.

MIAMI BEACH TROLLEY TOUR

Miami's Old Town Trolley Tour now extends to Miami Beach. You can pick up the trolley at a sign on Ocean Drive at the junction with 11th Street. The trolley stops at the Holocaust Memorial, the Eden Roc Hotel (for public beaches and the boardwalk), and the Lincoln Road Mall (for the Art Center), before turning back to Bayside Marketplace. This tour is two-hourly, not so good for hopping on and off.

Bayside Marketplace. Tel: (305) 374–8687. Tours: 11.05am–5.05pm (at Ocean Drive). Admission charge.

NIKKO GOLD COAST CRUISES

For a sea view of South Florida, try a cruise through Biscayne Bay passing 'Millionaires' Row' (the bayside homes of the rich and famous), Bayside Marketplace, Miami Seaquarium and Vizcaya.

Haulover Marina, 10800 Collins Avenue. Reservations – tel: (305) 945–5461. Open: 8.30am–9pm year round. Admission charge.

SOUTH POINTE

In the early 1900s, South Pointe was the hotspot of Miami Beach, with two casinos and some of the first hotels. It was also the birthplace of the Miami Chamber of Commerce and home of the city's first synagogue, the Congregation Beth Jacob. Historic landmarks include the Hotel Leonard and the Century Hotel, Deco Plaza, and Joe's Stone Crab Restaurant.

Just on the beach side of the MacArthur Causeway, look out for the pink and turquoise Art Deco elementary school. As the Beach's average age has dropped dramatically, it is the first school built in 20 years.

South Pointe Park, surrounded by

Bayside Marketplace – port of call on a Gold Coast cruise

water on three sides, is the best place to watch the cruise liners coming and going into and out of the Port of Miami, the world's largest cruise ship port, and the colourful tracks of the smaller craft against the brilliance of the sea.

The Everglades and Biscayne National Parks

*T*hough both depend on the water for their distinctive landscape and thriving wildlife, the Everglades and Biscayne national parks are completely different, though equally fascinating.

THE EVERGLADES

This is the last remaining American subtropical wilderness, where tropical life from the Caribbean blends with temperate species to form a rich sanctuary. Flowing through it is a strange freshwater river, only six inches deep but 50 miles wide, nicknamed the 'River of Grass'. There are spindly pines, hammocks of tropical hardwoods, luxuriant mosses, ferns and unexpected flowers, and the ubiquitous sawgrass. Birds are everywhere and the animals are wild and free; alligators move fast, and eat what they catch, so it is best to view them from the safety of an airboat.

Through the Everglades

The main entrance and visitor centre are some 10 miles southwest of Homestead on SR 9336. The only park road from here is a 38-mile drive south, without stops, to Flamingo on Florida Bay. The Pa-hay-okee Observation Tower, just off the main road, has a wide view of the River of Grass. The Anhinga Trail and the Gumbo-Limbo Trail, both located at the Royal Palm Visitor Center, just inside the national park, are the two most popular trails. On the half-mile Anhinga Trail, alligators, turtles and several species of fish and birds live below the boardwalks that cross the slough (waterhole).

Canoeing the wilderness waterway

A 99-mile canoe trail twists north from Flamingo to Everglades City, via the endless Gulf Coast marine and estuarine area. Paddle slowly to take in the surroundings.

Florida Bay

Best explored by boat, its tiny islands are refuges for nesting birds such as flamingos, spoonbills, ospreys, and the ubiquitous brown pelicans. Boat tours start at Flamingo Visitor Center.

BISCAYNE NATIONAL PARK

This watery world of coral reef, cobalt seas and long narrow keys is America's only aquatic national park. The entrance is 9 miles east of Homestead, at Convoy Point on North Canal Road (SW 328th Street). Many simply sail in. Boats scull gently over the sheltered surface of the Biscayne National Park, stopping to watch birds at tiny keys, and pausing to allow divers to explore coral reefs. The wrecks of old sailing ships, victims of storm or piracy, are perfect for snorkellers and scuba divers.

If you would rather keep your feet dry, take one of the daily 3-hour glass-bottom boat tours. There are also ranger-led tours and private sightseeing boats. Book through Biscayne Aqua Center (tel: (305) 247–2400).

EVERGLADES NATIONAL PARK

Main Visitor Centre, Royal Palm, 40001
SR9336, Homestead, FL33034–6733. Tel: (305)
242–7700. Main entrance – open all year round.
Two campgrounds, also overnight camping in
back (wild) country, permits required.

Admission charge.

BISCAYNE NATIONAL PARK

Ranger stations on Elliott Key and Adams Key.
PO Box 1369, Homestead, FL 33090.
Tel: Freephone (305) 247–PARK (main
entrance). Open: 8.00am–sunset.

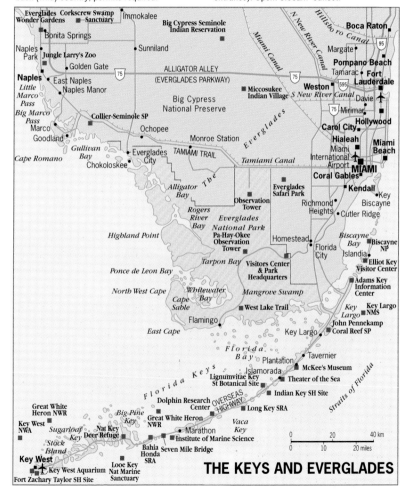

THE KEYS AND EVERGLADES

FLORIDA RARITIES

Florida is at the very south of the temperate zone, only a few degrees north of the Tropic of Capricorn and the tropical life of the Caribbean. The result is a rich mixture of temperate plants and animals, and many tropical birds and plants which have flown or blown across the sea from the Caribbean, to colonise wild places.

For most people, the greatest thrill is the extremely rare sight of a Florida panther, now on the endangered list. At around 60 to 130 pounds, it's the state's largest wild cat, a relative of the puma. Today, only some 50 or so panthers are hanging on by their claws, mostly in the Everglades or the Big Cypress area.

Almost as rare are the tiny Key deer, which are no larger than a medium-sized dog. Once plentiful along the Keys, they now live mostly in a wildlife refuge on Big Pine Key, though you may see them elsewhere. If you do, don't be tempted to feed them. Reduced in number to less than 500, they are lured by food to dangerous roads, and they don't benefit from junk food, even if they like it.

If you see a large brown squirrel dashing up one of the mature pines or cypresses anywhere near Big Cypress National Preserve, it is likely to be a mangrove fox squirrel. It has a black head and back and an orange colour on its sides and tail.

The main danger to the manatee (sea

Feeding time for these manatees at Homosassa Springs

cow) is being cut by a boat's propeller. Today, there are only around 2,000 of these gentle giants left. Many manatees spend at least part of the winter in the warm waters of refuges and springs such as Blue Springs State Park or Port Everglades at Fort Lauderdale. Florida's natural resources are constantly under pressure, and the whole ecological balance of the Everglades is under serious threat as year by year many more of the state's waters are drained and unique land lost to building. These rarities too could join many others, like the Florida red wolf, now extinct.

Attractive hibiscus – typical of Florida's spectacular flora

Key deer can sometimes be glimpsed on Big Pine Key – their last stronghold

The glorious colours of bougainvillaea

The Keys

*T*he Florida Keys stretch 155 miles southwest from Miami to Key West, a wonderful drive with much to see *en route*. The road is rarely out of sight of the Gulf of Mexico on one side and the Atlantic on the other. The islands, some just tiny mangrove swamps, are haunts of rare animals, fish and birds with a host of wildlife refuges. The greatest attractions, however, often lie underwater where reefs, rocks and wrecks provide ideal conditions for fishing, sailing and diving.

A road with a view

There are 42 bridges between the islands – one alone is seven miles long – yet, so interwoven are land and sea that sometimes you hardly realise you are over water. All follow the track of Henry Flagler's astonishing 'railroad that went to the sea'. Built in 1912, it was destroyed by a hurricane in 1935.

In 1513, that diligent adventurer Ponce de León discovered the Florida Keys and named them *Los Mártires* (The Martyrs) because 'the rocks appeared like men who were suffering'.

Bahia Honda (meaning deep bay) is arguably the best of the Keys beaches

Piracy and wrecking

As pirates took over in the early 19th century, Key West became the fledgling US Navy's first station. Settlers followed and the native Indian Calusas gradually died out. Many things have combined to make the Keys what they are today. The first crops were the famous Key West limes, pineapples, breadfruit and tamarinds. Sharks were caught and their skin made into tough leather shagreen,

Cubans came to manufacture cigars, and gathering and selling sponges was big business. The honest trade of 'wrecking' (salvage) flourished, though it is also said that one or two Keys salvagers were not above 'helping' the occasional ship on to the rocks. With Flagler's railroad came the wealthy sun-seekers, and Key West became one of the richest cities in Florida.

Disaster and recovery

But prosperity did not last. In 1934 the Keys local authority had been forced to sign over its powers in exchange for Federal help. The plan was that sun, sea and climate could be put to use in tourism. The Great 1935 Hurricane that destroyed the Keys railway was the final blow to an economy battered by the Depression. Then came the war, in the event a turning point. Immediately after, the US Navy discovered 'pink gold', a particularly juicy variety of Keys shrimp. Today, more than one-and-a-quarter million visitors come to this unique area every year.

Key by Key

The long chain of Keys divides into three parts, Upper, Middle and Lower, each with its own atmosphere and attractions, though nearly all are based around the water – sailing, fishing, diving, swimming or snorkelling.

THE UPPER KEYS

The principal island groupings are: Key Largo, which includes Tavernier, named after an 18th-century pirate; and Islamorada, named 'the purple isles' because of their violet-coloured sea snails.

THE MIDDLE KEYS

Marathon is the biggest of a group of islands which takes in Conch, Duck, Grassy and Pigeon Keys. It is famous for its Seven-Mile Bridge to the Lower Keys.

THE LOWER KEYS TO KEY WEST

Key West is the target for most visitors who get this far, right at the end of the chain. But along the way are Bahia Honda, which boasts one of the best beaches in the Keys; Looe Key, a national marine sanctuary; and Big Pine, which is famous for its unique deer.

MILE MARKERS

Every mile from Florida City to Key West is counted off by a milemarker (MM) on the right-hand side of US1. Marker 126 (MM 126) stands just south of Florida City, MM 0 stands at the corner of Fleming and Whitehead streets in Key West. Keys people always use them when giving directions.

The Florida Keys – idyllic coral islands

The Keys

THE UPPER KEYS

Key Largo is just over an hour from Miami and is also handy for the Everglades across Florida Bay. The John Pennekamp Coral Reef State Park (MM 102.5) offers glass-bottom boat tours to show its 55 varieties of coral, more than 500 species of fish, and other rarely seen sealife. Further out is the Key Largo National Marine Sanctuary (MM 100) where divers and snorkellers can find the statue of *Christ of the Deep*, a 9-foot-tall bronze deliberately submerged in 25 feet of water off Dry Rocks Reef. Key Largo Marine Park is another underwater park and includes the Jules' Undersea Lodge. This is the world's first underwater hotel, which can accommodate six guests. Also at Key Largo is the original *African Queen* steamboat from the Bogart–Hepburn film of the same name. It is moored at the Holiday Inn resort (MM 100, Oceanside) and occasionally steams out for rides.

Tavernier is the jumping-off point for birdwatching tours of the Florida Bay Rookeries. The Harry Harris Park (MM 92.6) has a natural saltwater pool, a wonderful sandy beach and barbecue and picnic spots.

Islamorada is former President George Bush's favourite fishing area and has long been known as the sport fishing capital of the Keys. The Theater of the Sea (MM 84.5) features glass-bottom boats, tame dolphins, sharks and sea lions in (separate!) coral pools. You can swim with a dolphin and take part in a live show. Lignumvitae State Botanical Site (MM 78.5), preserves virgin tropical hardwoods, a glimpse of the ancient Keys. Indian Key (MM 79), on the Atlantic side, holds the ruined headquarters of some notable 19th-century wreckers (salvagers). Offshore, the wreck of the Spanish treasure ship *San Pedro* is rich in historic objects, and a haven for marine life. Long Key is good for snorkelling, and diving shops offer trips to nearby reefs. Long Key State Recreational Area (MM 67.5) has one of the Keys' best natural beaches and there are nature trails to its hardwood hammocks.

THE MIDDLE KEYS

Marathon is the mid-point of the Keys, a good base for east and west. It has one of the few Keys golf courses, an 18-hole public course (MM 50), and some fine natural attractions. The Dolphin Research Center (MM 59) on Grassy Key offers tours to help our under-standing of dolphins, and Crane Point Hammock (MM 50) is a 63-acre wilderness sanctuary, which has also revealed pre-Columbus remains and prehistoric Bahamian relics on the site of an Indian village. A new million-dollar museum, the Museum of Natural History of the Florida Keys, brings this

The original *African Queen*, at Key Largo

John Pennekamp Coral Reef State Park

unique area to life. At the south end of Marathon Key is the start of the Seven Mile Bridge and, adjacent, its predecessor which was partly destroyed in the hurricane of 1935.

THE LOWER KEYS

West of the Seven Mile Bridge is Bahia Honda Key, Florida's southernmost recreation area (MM 37).The sandy beach here is the best in the Keys, while the Silver Palm nature trail will show you rare West Indian flora found nowhere else in these islands. Big Pine Key is home to the tiny Key deer, once plentiful throughout the Keys; most now live in the safety of the National Key Deer Wildlife Refuge just north of US1. Close by is the Great White Heron National Wildlife Refuge, and to the south of the island is Looe Key National Marine Sanctuary, a diver's delight with staghorn, brain and elkhorn coral reefs. The old Bat Tower (MM 17) on Sugarloaf Key was built to attract mosquito-eating bats to feed on the voracious local pests!

PRESIDENTS' CHOICE

George Bush is not the only US President who loves the Keys. Harry S Truman spent so much time in Key West, that his holiday home became known as the 'Little White House'. President Dwight D Eisenhower convalesced there after a heart attack, and other presidential visitors included Richard Nixon and Franklin D Roosevelt.

Theater of the Sea

Tel: (305) 664–2431. Guided tours.

Open: 9.30am–4pm. Admission charge.

Dolphin Research Center

Tel: (305) 289–0002. Guided tours.

Open: 9am–4pm. Closed: Monday and Tuesday. Admission charge.

Museum of Natural History of the Florida Keys and Crane Point Hammock

Tel: (305) 743–3900. Open: Monday to Saturday 9am–5pm, Sunday noon–5pm. Admission charge.

HEMINGWAY IN KEY WEST

The Nobel prizewinner Ernest Hemingway wrote some of his best-known novels, including *A Farewell to Arms* and *For Whom the Bell Tolls*, in a loft over the Carriage House at his Key West home. He reached it by a catwalk from the main house's back balcony. Hemingway's schedule ran from 6am to noon, 500 words a day, and he did not set off for his favourite watering hole until he had finished writing.

After noon 'Papa' went along to meet his cronies in Sloppy Joe's, on Duval Street, much featured in the week-long Hemingway celebrations in July, where few of the revellers realise that it is no longer the original, which is now trading as Captain Tony's.

In the long afternoons, the writer would sail and fish in his boat, *Pilar*, which lies impounded in Cuba after Castro gave Hemingway his marching orders some 30 years later.

Today, luckily for the thousands of visitors who tour the 1851 Spanish Colonial-style house, where Hemingway and his second wife, Pauline, lived with their two sons, there is now a steep but conventional stairway up to the loft. The small hall gives a view of the

The original Sloppy Joe's

Come midday, after writing, the author would make his way to Sloppy Joe's

The courtyard – with cat – of Hemingway's much-visited home

Descendants of Hemingway's six-toed cats roam around the grounds in their dozens, to the delight of the visitors

The bedroom at Hemingway's house

simple, workmanlike room with a poster of the bullfighter José Luis Segura, and a table holding an ancient typewriter.

The house features the first salt-water swimming pool to be built in Key West. It took a year to complete, with 20 Cubans hand-digging out the sheer coral. It cost the staggering sum of $20,000, $12,000 more than he paid for the house.

Around this pool linger some 50 descendants of Hemingway's rare cats, all with extra toes – six on the front paws, five on the back which give them a strange club-footed walk. The original cats' ancestors were ships' cats which came ashore because, like Hemingway, they found the Keys a congenial place to live.

Key West

*K*ey West is the undisputed honeypot of the Keys. It measures only four miles by two miles so sightseeing is very easy. You can put the car away and either walk or use a bicycle or moped (both available for hire). The streets are narrow and tree-shaded and full of timber-framed houses with elaborate gingerbread-style decoration cut into their wooden trims.

Key West is a hotchpotch of many historical influences; Spanish colonists, British settlers fleeing American independence, Bahamian immigrants, and more. Today, locals and visitors alike value its quiet retreat and sea pastimes.

It is an outpost, away from the mainland but, since the Civil War, the main base of the US Navy's Caribbean Basin Fleet. The Navy has earned its right to be here. In the late 1940s, it not only brought in the first fresh water but navy divers also discovered the lucrative 'pink gold', the Gulf shrimp, that gave new prosperity to the Keys.

A TOUR OF KEY WEST

There are two ways of getting an introduction to Key West. The Conch Tour Train runs a historical 90-minute tour that blends old and new Key West, and the Old Town Trolley Tour covers 18 miles and 125 points of interest, also in 90 minutes, with 12 brief stops (see also walk on pages 26–7).
Conch Tour Trains – 301 Front Street. Tel: (305) 294–5161. Open: 9am–4pm. Old Town Trolley – 1910 N Roosevelt Boulevard. Tel: (305) 296–6688. Open: 8.55am–4.30pm.

AUDUBON HOUSE AND GARDENS

This old mansion is named after the renowned naturalist and bird artist, John James Audubon, who painted in Key West during his 1832 Florida expedition. Notice the four beautiful Audubon bird prints on the first landing.

The unpretentious Audubon House

The home of seaman and ship salvager Captain John H Geiger, it also includes the Geiger Gallery and 18th- and 19th-century furniture.
Whitehead Street and Greene Street.
Tel: (305) 296–2116. Guided tours. Open:
9.30am–5pm daily. Admission charge.

EAST MARTELLO TOWER MUSEUM AND GALLERY

Military strategists will appreciate the clever triangular defence system of this fort. This brick building is packed with historical and military exhibits and has a gallery containing Keys artefacts.
3501 S Roosevelt Boulevard. Tel: (305)
296–3913. Guided tours. Open:
9.30am–5.30pm daily.

ERNEST HEMINGWAY HOUSE

The writer first came to Key West in 1929, and lived in this 1851 house from 1931 to 1942. Surrounded by furnishings brought from Spain, Cuba and Africa, Hemingway owned Key West's first bathroom. Here he wrote some of his most important works. There is a penny embedded in the patio of the pool, placed there when he gave his 'last penny' to pay for it!
907 Whitehead Street. Tel: (305)
294–1575. Guided tours. Open: 9am–5pm.
Admission charge.

FORT ZACHARY TAYLOR STATE HISTORIC SITE

Once on an offshore shoal, now landlocked, Fort Zachary Taylor (part of the defence chain), a three-storey fortification built between 1845 and 1866, was lying almost forgotten under the sand. Now it has one of the largest Civil War cannon displays in the United States. An enthusiastic volunteer group has also excavated a buried

Fabric being screen printed by hand

arsenal, now on view, from the Keys' turbulent past and holds re-enactments of events.
Southard Street in Truman Annex.
Tel: (305) 292–6713. Guided Tours.
Open: 8am–sunset. Admission charge.

KEY WEST AQUARIUM

One of the first open-air aquariums when it opened, this has a large collection of all forms of sea life, including tropical fish.
1 Whitehead Street. Tel: (305) 296–2051.
Guided tours. Open: 10am–6pm daily.
Admission charge.

KEY WEST HAND PRINT FABRICS

Here you can see fabrics designed, screen-printed, and sewn to make tropical-coloured garments, in the Curry Warehouse, once an old tobacco warehouse. Next door is a shop where you can browse and buy garments.
201 Simonton Street. Tel: (305)
294–9535. Open: 10am–6pm daily.

Key West lighthouse, now a museum

KEY WEST LIGHTHOUSE

With some 90 or so spiral steps up to the top it is well worth the climb for the brilliant view of palm shores and sparkling sea. In 1848, this lighthouse replaced an earlier one destroyed by the 1846 hurricane. Oddly for those times, Key West had two women lighthouse keepers: Barbara Mabritt from 1832 to the Civil War, and Mary Bethel, who succeeded her husband from 1908 to 1914. A delightful museum details these and other fascinating facts.
938 Whitehead Street. Tel: (305) 294–0012. Guided tours. Open: 9.30am–5pm. Admission charge.

KEY WEST SEAPLANES

This is the quickest way to the Dry Tortugas (Tortoise) islands, 70 miles west and famous for wildlife, and also to Fort Jefferson National Monument. On the way you can see sharks, frigate birds, rays and wrecks, including the treasure site of the *Atocha*.
5603 W Junior College Road. For departure times – tel: (305) 294–6978.

LITTLE WHITE HOUSE

This was President Harry S Truman's hideaway during his six years in office, faithfully restored both inside and out, with a 2-acre garden.
111 Front Street, Truman Annex. Tel: (305) 294–9911. Open: daily 9am–5pm. Admission charge.

MALLORY SQUARE AND WATERFRONT

The historic waterfront and streets near by form this part of town: cafés, museums, theatres, shops and the start of Key West tours. The waterfront attracts a celebratory crowd at sunset to cheer the sun down, with jugglers, tumblers, an escapologist, even a Scots bagpiper, and an abiding scent of hot popcorn curiously mixed with frying onions.
Main shopping hours: 10am–6pm.

MEL FISHER MARITIME HERITAGE SOCIETY

The museum has gold, silver and other dazzling treasure salvaged by Mel Fisher, the best-known treasure seeker in Florida. In 1969 his team discovered the galleons *Nuestra Senhora de Atocha* and the *Santa Margarita* which sank in a hurricane in 1622, loaded with royal and private treasures. It took a further 16 years to salvage all the riches, and finds from the ships are exhibited in the museum. For children there is the Discovery Corner, with Spanish costumes.

200 Greene Street. Tel: (305) 294–2633. Open: 9.30am–5pm. Admission charge.

REEF CRUISER *FIREBALL*

A two-hour trip out to see brilliantly coloured fish, sea fans, plumes and the only living coral reef in the continental US. Upper- and lower-deck viewing from a glass-bottom boat. Best at sunset. Many other boats on offer.

Fireball Dock, 2 Duval Street. For reservations and tickets – tel: (305) 296–6293.

REEF RELIEF ENVIRONMENTAL CENTER

This non-profit-making centre is dedicated to preserving the living coral reef.

201 William Street. Tel: (305) 294–3100. Open: Monday to Saturday 9am–5pm. Free.

ST PAUL'S CHURCH

Hurricane and fire have taken their toll on St Paul's and this is the fourth church on this site. The first was built in 1832, which makes this Florida's oldest Episcopal church. The present building dates from 1919. The best time to visit is the hour before sunset, when the sun lights the stained-glass window above the door, and the 15 windows inside are each sunlit in turn. The church bell heralds the sunset.

Sunday Services: 7.30 am, 9am, also 11.00am January to Palm Sunday. Open: daily, except during services.

TURTLE KRAALS

A well-known landmark in the shrimp dock area at the end of Key West Bight, the Kraals show loggerhead turtles close up, some as big as 400 pounds. There is also a touch tank where children can feel harmless sea creatures, and an aviary.

2 Land's End Village. Tel: (305) 294–2640. Open: 11am–1am daily. Free.

WRECKERS' MUSEUM

This is the oldest house in Key West and was once the home of a sea captain and his nine daughters. It has ship models, salvage documents, and a wonderful old doll's house.

322 Duval Street. Tel: (305) 294–9502. Guided tours. Open: 10am–4pm. Admission charge.

Treasures in the Wreckers' Museum

FLORIDA
FESTIVALS

Floridians love festivals, not just the sort of manufactured festival designed to entertain visitors, but the true ethnic celebration that has grown out of Florida's way of life, both past and present.

Calle Ocho hosts a huge street party in Little Havana, which is the culmination of nine days of Carnaval Miami, the biggest Hispanic festival in the US. In June, the Goombay Festival in Miami's Coconut Grove emphasises Bahamian influence. Ybor City, the Cuban quarter in Tampa, celebrates Hallowe'en with Latin-style verve and a colourful parade.

Torchlight processions through St Augustine's Spanish Quarter, British Colonial customs, and carols herald Christmas, as do the town's Grand Illuminations. St Augustine also has the Easter Festival and Passion Play with celebrations from Palm Sunday to Easter weekend. Another festival with religious significance is the Festival of the Epiphany, in the Greek community at Tarpon Springs on the west coast, a Greek Orthodox observance of Christ's baptism. The high spot is the blessing of the sponge fleet, and the whole festival is a blend of Greek music, dancing and food.

You are more likely to get a first sound rather than a first sight of the International Carillon Festival, as musicians play the 57-bell carillon from a keyboard inside the 205-foot tower in Bok Tower Gardens, at Lake Wales, south of Orlando. St Petersburg's Festival of the States is even more *fortissimo*, with high-school bands from the whole

Every Easter another colourful parade enlivens the streets of St Augustine

St Augustine's
December boat
parade

nation; and, in May, West Palm Beach jumps to the beat of Sunfest, the largest jazz festival in Florida.

But the most international of all is probably the Art Deco Weekend in January, in honour of this unique part of Miami Beach. It brings in architects and enthusiasts from all over the world to exchange ideas and feast their eyes on the styles, pastel shades and distinctive decoration of the Art Deco buildings of this historic area.

Jacksonville Jazz Festival – a huge event held at Metropolitan Park

Live music at Calle
Ocho, Little Havana

Southwest Gold Coast

*T*hey call this coast Florida's Florida: islands, palms and a moon to turn the sand silver-white. Next morning, the shellers are out at dawn to see what the last tide has brought in. The extreme south lies just on the edge of the Everglades, and the excursions and trails on this side of the coast are every bit as interesting as the more trodden paths into the 'glades on the east coast, with tours aplenty. From Fort Lauderdale, Alligator Way cuts through the Seminole Indian Reservation (SR 84) to cross the northern edge of the Everglades.

White gold

Naples, founded by a nostalgic Confederate veteran who had once served the King of Naples, is an attractive, understated, wealthy resort. Further north, the Lee Island Coast edged by white-gold sand is sheltered by islands such as Sanibel and Captiva, the mecca for shellers. Inland, Bonita Springs is a miniature Everglades.

Fort Myers, split into north and south by the Caloosahatchee River, was made famous by the arrival of the inventor Thomas Edison, who, with his friends and business associates Harvey Firestone and Henry Ford, worked here on his many inventions.

Boardwalk at Corkscrew Swamp Sanctuary

Near by is Estero Island, and Fort Myers Beach is ideal for families. All along this coast are numerous diving, fishing, sailing, and snorkelling opportunities. Cape Coral has extensive inland waterways – more canals than Venice – and also some of Florida's best golf courses. Sarasota is the most attractive city on this coast. It was supposedly named after the daughter of conquistador Hernando de Soto, who came in search of gold.

NAPLES AND THE NORTH

CARIBBEAN GARDENS

Wander through 52 acres of luscious botanical and zoological gardens: safari cruises, tram tours, lectures, elephant rides, playgrounds etc.
1590 Goodlette-Frank Road, Naples. Tel: (813) 262–5409.

COLLIER COUNTY MUSEUM

Here you will find the history of Collier County from prehistoric times to the present. A 2-acre historical park features a Seminole Village, and a steam locomotive.
3301 Tamiami Trail East, Naples. Tel: (813) 774–8476. Open: Monday to Friday 9am–5pm. Free.

CORKSCREW SWAMP SANCTUARY

The Audubon Society's Boardwalk Trail through the cypress forest gives good views of alligators and other wildlife. The sanctuary contains the largest known stand of virgin bald cypress in eastern North America, which includes trees over 500 years old and up to 100 feet tall.

Immokalee Road (CR 846), 20 miles east of Naples. Tel: (813) 657–3771. Guided tours. Open: 9am–5pm daily. Admission charge.

FRANNIE'S TEDDY BEAR MUSEUM

Kids and enthusiasts will love the 1,800 bears from all over the world.

2511 Pine Ridge Road, Naples. Tel: (813) 598–2711. Open: Wednesday to Saturday 10am–5pm, Sunday 1–5pm. Admission charge.

THE LEE ISLAND COAST AND ISLANDS

CRUISING FROM CAPTIVA

Much of the beauty of this coast can only be appreciated from the water. Breakfast cruises depart daily at 9am.

Cruises from the Gulf, South Seas Plantation, Captiva. For times and reservations – tel: (813) 472–7549.

EDEN VINEYARDS WINERYAND PARK TOURS

Sample the 'southernmost' wine in the US by taking the tour of the vineyard and park grounds.

10 miles east of Fort Myers off I–75, exit 25. 19850 State Road 80, Alva. Tel: (813) 728–WINE. Open: 11am–5pm. Nominal charge.

EDISON WINTER HOME

Thomas Edison made Fort Myers his winter home in 1886, and his major achievement here was the development of rubber from the goldenrod plant. The laboratory holds its original equipment Edison used for his research from 1925 to 1931.

2350 McGregor Boulevard, Fort Myers. Tel: (813) 334–3614. Tours of house, garden and museum. Open: Monday to Saturday 9am–4pm, Sunday 12.30–4pm. Admission charge.

EVERGLADES WONDER GARDENS

This small zoo-garden of Everglades wildlife is the area's oldest attraction, with the elusive Florida panther, Big Joe the 1,000-pound saltwater crocodile and some amusing Everglades river otters.

On Old US 41 (SR 887), Bonita Springs. Tel: (813) 992–2591. Open: 9.30am–5pm daily. Admission charge.

SANIBEL SEA SHELLS

On Sanibel Island, they call it the 'Sanibel Stoop', on Captiva, it's the 'Captiva Crouch' – the characteristic bending forward that distinguishes the true sheller, people who spend their waking hours combing these beautiful beaches for rare treasures. Many have enormous collections and there are special shelling boat tours. There are restrictions, however. You may only take a maximum of two live shells per species and penalties are severe. Call at the islands' tourist information centre for details.

J N 'DING' DARLING WILDLIFE REFUGE

This is a feast for experts and the general public, a 5-mile Wildlife Drive past alligators, roseate spoonbills and great egrets. There are also three walking trails and two canoe trails.

Sanibel/Captiva Road. Tel: (813) 472–1100. Open: sunrise-sunset, except Friday. Admission charge. Special canoe and guided tours from Tarpon Bay Canoe Rentals inside Refuge – tel: (813) 472–8900.

MUSEUM OF THE ISLANDS

The life of the original inhabitants, the Calusa Indians, is explained through artefacts and displays, including an Indian dugout canoe.

Corner Russell Rd/Sesame Drive, Pine Island. Tel: (813) 283–1525. Open: 10am–4.30pm daily. Free.

NATURE CENTER OF LEE COUNTY AND PLANETARIUM

A boardwalk tour of natural Florida, a planetarium show, and an Audubon aviary.

3450 Ortiz Avenue, Fort Myers. Tel: (813) 275–3616. Guided tours. Open: Monday to Saturday 9am–4pm, Sunday 11am–4.30pm. Admission charge.

SEMINOLE GULF RAILWAY

Board an elegant old train and enjoy the sights of Southwest Florida's subtropical terrain over lunch or dinner.

Metro Mall Station, Colonial Boulevard, Fort Myers. Times/reservations, tel: (813) 275–8487.

SHELL FACTORY

A 50-year-old institution which has a huge collection of shells, coral and sponges for sale.

2787 North Tamiami Trail, North Fort Myers. Tel: (813) 995–2141. Open: 9am–6.30pm, Sunday 10am–6pm. Free.

SUNBURST TROPICAL FRUIT COMPANY

Tour one of the state's oldest mango groves (dating from the 1920s) in a converted mango-picking trailer, then sample this delicious fruit.

7113 Road, Bokeelia. Reservations essential. Tel: (813) 283–1200. Admission charge.

TALL SHIP *EAGLE*

Get a feel for the past in the 68-foot topsail schooner *Eagle*. Daily excursions, monthly trip to Key West and weekend trips to Cabbage Key.

Getaway Marina, 18400 San Carlos Boulevard, Fort Myers Beach. Times and reservations, tel: (813) 466–3600; after 5pm (813) 466–SEAS.

Named after the sinuous creek snaking through it, the Corkscrew Swamp Sanctuary harbours alligators, otters and a huge collection of wood storks

SARASOTA

MARIE SELBY BOTANICAL GARDENS

These gardens are among the state's finest; the star attraction is the collection of over 6,000 orchids, among some 20,000 greenhouse plants, plus thousands more outside.
811 South Palm Avenue, Sarasota. Tel: (813) 366–5730. Open: daily 10am–5pm. Admission charge.

RINGLING MUSEUM OF ART

Florida's State Museum of Art is one of the finest and largest collections of European paintings in America. The sumptuous Italian Renaissance-style villa in which it is housed is a visual delight.
5401 Bay Shore Road. Tel: (813) 355–5101. Guided tours. Open: 10am–5.30pm. Admission charge.

BRADENTON

BRADEN CASTLE PARK

The ruins of an old plantation house stand on a lovely site at the junction of the Braden and Manatee rivers and enjoy fine views.
1 Office Drive. Tel (313) 746–7700. Open: sunrise to sunset. Free.

MANATEE VILLAGE HISTORICAL PARK

On the National Register of Historic Places, the park offers vivid reminders of Manatee's past with five historic buildings, including the Court House and a one-room schoolhouse.
604 15th Street East. Tel: (813) 749–7165. Guided tours. Open: Monday to Saturday 9am–4pm, Sunday 2–5pm. Closed: summer Sundays. Free.

Ellzey

Kendrick

Cedar Key

Waccasassa Bay

Yankeetown

Dunnellon Ocala

Crystal River

Lake Tsala 75

Homosassa Springs SWP   Inverness *Lake Apopka*

Weeki Wachee Spring

Bushnell

Hernando

Brooksville

Beach

Hudson

Ridge Manor

Port Richey

Pasco

Dade City

Lutz

Tarpon

Zephyrhills

Spongeorama Springs

Honeymoon I   Dunedin

275

Busch Gardens 4

Caladesi I

Clearwater *Old Tampa*

Madeira Largo *Bay* TAMPA Brandon

Lakeland

Beach

Treasure Sunken

Island Gardens

St Petersburg ST PETERSBURG

Bartow

Beach *Tampa* Wimauma

Fort De *Bay* 75

Soto Park

Fort Meade

Parrish

De Soto Nat Mem

Bradenton

Wauchula

Longboat Key

Ringling Museum

Sarasota Fruitville

Zolfo Springs

Osprey

Myakka River SP

Venice 75 Nocatee Arcadia

Englewood

Port Charlotte

Grove City

Punta Gorda

Charlotte Harbor

North Fort Myers

Pine Island Bokeelia Cape

Nat Wildlife Coral

Refuge

Captiva I Fort Myers

Sanibel I Fort Myers

JN "Ding" Darling NWR Beach

Everglades Wonder Gardens

Bonita Corkscrew

Springs Swamp

0   20   40 km Sanctuary

0   10   20 miles

Naples East Naples

WEST COAST

ORANGES AND LEMONS

Florida must be the only place in the world that has orange juice as its official drink, and citrus fruits, mostly oranges, tangerines and grapefruit, are the state's most important agricultural industry. In the early 1880s, there were more than 70 million citrus trees in the Florida groves.

The Spanish brought oranges to Florida in the late 16th century, but it was not until over 200 years later that the crop was commercially exploited. The man who usually gets the credit for planting the first commercial citrus grove is the French count, Odet Philippe. Today, one of the oldest groves in Florida still in cultivation is the Don Philippe Grove in Pinellas County, planted in the early 1800s.

The citrus groves have been devastated three times by frost: in the late 1800s, again in the early 1970s and latterly in the 1980s.

In the early 1880s there were more than 70 million citrus trees in the state, but the peak production year was in 1979 when Florida produced 2 billion boxes, for juice as well as to eat whole. Today, citrus processing and the freezing of orange juice are as important as citrus growing.

According to Florida folklore an orange blossom led to the founding of the great city of Miami, through the enterprise of Julia Tuttle, who owned land on the north bank of the Miami River. Her pleas to Henry Flagler to extend his railway south from Palm Beach were in vain until she sent him freshly picked orange blossoms to prove that Miami had escaped the ferocious frost. The great entrepreneur was thus convinced of Miami's tourism potential.

The Florida Citrus Tower at Clermont, in hilly country west of Orlando, is the best place to learn about the citrus fruit industry in more detail.

The state produces millions of boxes of fruit for juice alone

Citrus groves are still the mainstay of Florida's agricultural industry

Grapefruits ripening in the sun

As might be expected, the quality of fruit at local markets is second to none

Tampa Bay and the Pinellas Suncoast

*T*he most exciting route into the Pinellas, also known as the St Petersburg Clearwater area, is across the four-mile-long Sunshine Skyway Bridge that connects Bradenton and the Pinellas. The name Pinellas comes from when the Spanish explorers first visited, and pines covered the area. They called it *punta pinal,* 'the point of the pines'.

The view from the bridge is dramatic: to the right, the bay with Tampa in the northeast corner, and St Petersburg, the 'capital' of the Pinellas. On the left are the five small keys that make up Fort DeSoto Park. The largest, Mullet Key, holds Fort DeSoto, named after the Spanish adventurer. These islands are a perfect haven for swimmers and sunbathers, with some of the west's best beaches.

Sand and palms

Once this coast was home to Tocabago Indians, and traces of their shell mounds and villages are still there. Today, its warm, clean sands, edged with palms, are bright with the colours of sun-loungers. Fishing piers angle out over the sparkling water of the Gulf of Mexico; apartment houses and hotels lie to landward. Often called the Suncoast, this 28-mile stretch takes in St Petersburg (St Pete's) Beach, Treasure Island, Madeira Beach, Indian Rocks Beach, and the busy resort of Clearwater. Dunedin indicates its Scottish origins by its very name, and Tarpon Springs is a community with very strong Greek links.

North of the Suncoast

Head north for some 45 miles to Homosassa Springs Wildlife Park, where manatees swim in a natural spring. Around 30 miles further north, Cedar Key is a sleepy, old-fashioned fishing village at the end of a 3-mile bridge.

Boatyard Village, a mock 1890s fishing village with lots of atmosphere

THE PINELLAS

SUNCOAST SEABIRD SANCTUARY

Ralph Heath founded this acclaimed sanctuary in 1971 after he came across an injured cormorant, and so became the Pinella's 'bird doctor'. The sanctuary has some 500 temporary and long-term residents.

18328 Gulf Boulevard, Indian Shores.
Tel: (813) 391–6211. Group tour.
Open: 9am–sunset. Free.

Antics at the Suncoast Seabird Sanctuary

BOATYARD VILLAGE

This atmospheric re-created 1890s
fishing village, set in a Tampa Bay cove,
has restaurants, boutiques, galleries and
a playhouse.
*16100 Fairchild Drive, Clearwater.
Tel: (813) 535–4678. Open: Monday to
Thursday 10am–7pm, Friday to Saturday
9pm, Sunday to 6pm. Free.*

CALADESI AND HONEYMOON
ISLANDS

Caladesi is one of the last undisturbed
barrier islands – perfect for swimming,
shelling, fishing, diving, and walking
along its 3-mile nature trail. It is reached
only by hourly boat from Dunedin,
Honeymoon Island or Clearwater.
Honeymoon Island got its name when
a developer built 50 thatched
'honeymoon' bungalows here. There's a
rare stand of original pine, long beaches,
and mangrove swamps.
Open: 8am–sunset. Contacts: Caladesi

*State Park, tel: (813) 443–5903. Boat
information and reservation: from
Honeymoon Island, tel: (813) 734–5263;
from Clearwater (813) 442–7433.
Honeymoon Island State Recreation Area,
tel: (813) 734–4255.*

EUROPA CRUISES

Cruises set out from Madeira Beach to
the Gulf of Mexico or the Atlantic
Ocean. Choose from cruises offering
Sunday brunch, a day cruise or an
evening's entertainment, including a
casino.
*150 153rd Avenue, Suite 202, Madeira
Beach. Times/reservations, tel: (813)
393–2885.*

FLORIDA MILITARY AVIATION
MUSEUM

This small outdoor museum has several
restored World War II aircraft and
aviation exhibits, plus military vehicles
and weapons systems. See also the
adjacent 94th Aero Squadron restaurant.
*Fairchild Avenue, near St Petersburg/
Clearwater Airport (off Highway 686).
Tel: (813) 584–6208. Tours: Tuesday,
Thursday, Saturday 10am–4pm, Sunday
1pm–5pm. Admission charge.*

More residents of the sanctuary

Spongeorama at Tarpon Springs

HERITAGE PARK AND MUSEUM

Discover early pioneer life among a fascinating collection of 14 of the county's oldest buildings, lovingly restored and transported lock, stock and barrel to this leafy park. Pioneer skills such as spinning and weaving are demonstrated.
11909 125th Street North, Largo. Tel: (813) 462–3474. Open: Tuesday to Saturday 10am–4pm, Sunday 1–4pm.

HOMOSASSA SPRINGS STATE WILDLIFE PARK

It's worth the one-hour drive north of the Pinellas to watch the Florida manatee in the wild. Visitors walk through an underwater observatory to see the 'gentle giants' and thousands of fish in a natural spring. There are also scenic cruises and nature trails, where you may spot alligators and crocodiles.
9925 W Fishbowl Drive, Homosassa (off US19/98). Tel: (904) 628–5343. Open: 9am–5.30pm. Admission charge.

JOHN'S PASS VILLAGE AND BOARDWALK

This charmingly restored fishermen's village of some 60 shaky-looking tin-roofed wooden shacks is home to galleries, shops, restaurants, and the John's Pass Seafood Festival in October.

A boardwalk oversees the comings and goings of the local fishing and charter fleet.
12901 Gulf Boulevard East, Madeira Beach. Tel: (813) 397–7242. Open: 10am–9pm (shops).

MARINE SCIENCE CENTER

The public are always welcome at this research and rehabilitation establishment for sea creatures. Stranded and injured sea mammals are cared for here and sometimes become long-term residents. Sunset Sam, the bottlenose dolphin, is the star of the centre.
249 Windward Passage, Clearwater. Tel: (813) 447–0980. Guided tours. Open: Monday to Friday 9am–5pm, Saturday 9am–4pm, Sunday 11am–4pm. Admission charge.

PHILIPPE PARK

This historical site overlooks Old Tampa Bay and is named after Count Odet Philippe, a surgeon in Napoleon's army who introduced the grapefruit to Florida. Centuries before, Tocabago Indians settled here and an Indian mound remains here today. This is a good spot for picnics.
2355 Bayshore Drive, Safety Harbor (north of St Petersburg). Tel: (813) 726–2700.

RAILROAD HISTORICAL MUSEUM

Mementoes from Dunedin's Scottish past are housed in this old 1889 Orange Belt Railroad station. Walking tours of Dunedin's historic area leave from here.
31 Main Street, Dunedin. Tel: (813) 733–4151. Open: Tuesday, Saturday 10am–noon, Thursday 9.30am–11.30am. Closed: June to 1 October.

ST NICHOLAS BOAT LINE

Learn how traditional Greek sponge divers ply their trade with a real diver in full Jules Verne-style diving suit at work under the water. Afterwards you can visit the sponge shop on the wharf.

693 Dodecanese Boulevard, Tarpon Springs. Tel: (813) 937–9887. Daily.

ST NICHOLAS GREEK ORTHODOX CATHEDRAL

Built in 1943 on the site of the simpler church raised by the first settlers, St Nicholas's is a replica of St Sophia in Istanbul. It has all the Byzantine opulence of an Orthodox church, with marble, stained glass and beautiful icons.

36 North Pinellas Avenue (Alt 19), Tarpon Springs. Tel (813) 937–3540. Guided tours. Open: 9am–5pm.

SILAS BAYSIDE MARKET

This is a small shopping village in a tropical setting with many speciality shops and a good food court.

Water fun at Weeki Wachee Spring

5505 Gulf Boulevard, St Petersburg Beach. Tel: (813) 367–4485. Open: daily.

SPONGEORAMA

This is an informal exhibition which explains the history of the town's sponge industry and its Greek community. Museum, theatre and gift shop.

510 Dodecanese Boulevard, Tarpon Springs. Tel: (813) 942–3771. Guided tours. Open: 10am–9pm. Admission charge.

WEEKI WACHEE SPRING

This nature theme park features an all-singing, all-dancing underwater mermaid show. Taking lungfuls of air from submerged air lines, the performers act out the adventures of Hans Andersen's *Little Mermaid*. The other highlight is the Wilderness River Cruise. Also water park and exotic bird shows.

US 19 (at SR 50), Brooksville. Tel: (904) 596–2062. Open: 10am–6pm.

St Petersburg and Tampa

Espíritu Santo

When Hernando de Soto first explored this area in 1539, he discovered five mineral springs in a large Tocabaga village north of St Petersburg, in what is now Safety Harbor. The natives believed that the springs had healing qualities, and so de Soto named the area La Bahía del Espíritu Santo, meaning the Bay of the Holy Spirit.

Over 300 years later, in 1885, the American Medical Association came to much the same conclusion about the region as a whole. That year they pronounced that the Pinellas boasted the ideal climate and location for a 'world health city' and even made reference to the area west of Tampa Bay where St Petersburg was just being founded.

The previous year, railroad magnate Henry Plant had brought his railroad into Tampa. Plant, however, was not the first man to bring the railroad into St

Busy St Petersburg Beach

Petersburg. That honour went to Peter Demens (Petrovich Demenshev) whose Orange Belt Railroad rolled into town in 1888. Local legend has it that Demens and John Williams – the city founder – drew lots for the honour of naming the new town. Demens won and called it St Petersburg after his home town in Russia. A few years later Henry Plant bought Demens' railroad. Visitors and tourists flocked in and, to accommodate them, Plant built the luxury Belleview Hotel in Clearwater. Recently renovated, and now known as the Belleview Mido, it still claims to be the world's largest occupied wooden structure. Another early hotel on this coast was the Don CeSar at St Petersburg Beach. Its pink stucco walls and turrets are still a famous landmark to guests from all over the world.

Early air travel
St Petersburg has the distinction of having inaugurated the first commercial passenger flight in America. In 1914 a sea plane called the *Benoist* flew the mayor from the city's waterfront to Tampa, 21 miles away. From today's pier you can still see and hear the weekend fliers taking off from Albert Whitted Airport, close to the water, though the area now has its own international airport, southeast of Clearwater.

ST PETERSBURG

BAYFRONT CENTER
This is the place for celebrity shows, theatrical productions, special exhibitions, athletics events and other performances.
5505 Gulf Boulevard. Tel: (813) 892–5767 for tickets and information.

BOYD HILL NATURE TRAIL
Six short nature walks and boardwalks, each lasting around 15 minutes, explore some of the 216 acres of natural subtropical habitat. Educational shows, day camps and bird walks are also on offer.
1101 Country Club Way South. Tel: (813) 893–7211. Guided tours. Open: 9am–5pm. Admission charge.

THE COLISEUM
The Coliseum Ballroom opened in 1924, at the period when ballroom dancing was at its height. Hundreds of big bands have played here and thousands of people have waltzed and tangoed on its huge expanse of shining maple dance floor.

535 Fourth Avenue North. Tel: (813) 894–1812. Dances are held at the Coliseum every Wednesday and Saturday.

GREAT EXPLORATIONS
See yourself reflected into infinity in this intriguing 'hands-on' museum, with lots of machines and puzzles that educate as well as entertain. Special exhibits include Phenomenal Arts, the Touch Tunnel and the Body Shop. Avoid weekday mornings when school trips arrive.
1120 Fourth Street South. Tel: (813) 821–8992. Open: Monday to Saturday 10am–5pm, Sunday noon–5pm. Admission charge.

Youngsters in particular find this fascinating museum great fun

MUSEUM OF FINE ARTS
The museum is noted for its excellent collection of French Impressionist paintings, but also has outstanding European, American, pre-Columbian and Far Eastern exhibits. Be sure to see the art photography collection by American masters (see page 35).
255 Beach Drive. Tel: (813) 896–2667. Guided tours. Open: Tuesday to Saturday 10am–5pm, Sunday 1–5pm, third Thursday of each month to 9pm. Admission charge.

THE PIER

The distinctive five-storey Pier, looking a bit like the stern of a huge ocean liner, is a well-known landmark on Florida's west coast. It has dining areas, shops, aquarium, fishing, boat rentals and more. For the best view, take a meal on the top observation deck, and see the Bay and Bayfront, and the weekend fliers across the water (see page 35).
800 Second Avenue NE. Tel: (813) 821–6164. Open: 10am–9pm, Sunday 11am–7pm.

ST PETERSBURG HISTORICAL AND FLIGHT ONE MUSEUM

Here you will find thousands of reminders of pioneer days, including china, glassware, coins, dolls, shells and pictures of early landmarks. The old newspaper clippings are particularly revealing. A replica of the Benoist seaplane is included, also changing exhibits on Florida and local history.
335 Second Avenue. Tel: (813) 894–1052. Open: Monday to Saturday 10am–5pm, Sunday 1–5pm. Admission charge.

The unusual pier at St Petersburg

ST PETERSBURG THUNDERDOME

Florida's first state-of-the-art domed stadium seats up to 43,000 people and hopes to attract major-league baseball to St Petersburg. It is currently a home to athletics events, concerts and other major spectator events. If no event is in progress you are welcome to look around inside.
1 Stadium Drive. Tel: (813) 825–3100 for information. Tours available on non-event days.

Masterpiece at the Dali Museum

SALVADOR DALI MUSEUM

This is a tribute to the great Spanish Surrealist painter, with the world's biggest collection of his works, including 93 oils and over 100 watercolours. Take at least two to three hours to absorb the paintings, sculptures, drawings, and Dali's collaborations with photographer Philippe Halsman, which resulted in some astonishing pictures, (at first, no one dared to publish them). Tours give a good background to the collection and staff point out interesting details (see page 35).

1000 Third Street South. Tel: (813) 823–3767. Guided tours. Open: Tuesday to Saturday 10am–5pm, Sunday noon–5pm. Admission charge.

THE SUNKEN GARDENS

This lush tropical five-acre garden in the centre of St Petersburg has more than 5,000 varieties of plants and over 500 exotic birds and animals. A walk through the aviary is a highlight.

1825 4th Street North. Tel: (813) 896–3186. Open: daily 9am–5.30pm. Admission charge.

TAMPA ON THE BAY

Tampa started life as an Indian fishing village visited by Hernando de Soto in 1539, though some historians claim that Ponce de León, the first European to discover Florida's east coast, also came to Tampa Bay in 1513. It was listed as an Indian settlement in 1580, when the name Tampa was heard for the first time. The meaning of this word is unclear and has been interpreted in various ways, from the prosaic 'town near the bay' to the poetic 'sticks of fire'. In 1823 Tampa became Fort Brooke and began to develop as a trading centre. Plant's railroad link in 1885 confirmed the city's stature (by now 'Tampa' again) and the following year Vicente Martinez Ybor successfully moved the Key West Cuban cigar-making industry to Tampa.

The coming of the railroad

By this time, Henry B Plant had brought his railroad to Tampa and, in competition with Flagler's fabulous east coast hotels, Plant spent the then-astronomical sum of $3 million on the

The Sunshine Skyway, just over four miles long, is a spectacular suspension bridge linking St Petersburg and Sarasota

Tampa Bay Hotel, which served even more rich visitors. Today, now part of the University of Tampa, its distinctive Moorish minarets still stand out against the Gulf Coast sunset.

Travel today

Today, Tampa International Airport, one of the most modern in the US, is fast becoming a front-runner as an entrance to Florida. For Tampa has the best of both worlds – the sands and brilliant, painted sunsets of the Gulf Coast on its doorstep, and the theme parks of Orlando just over an hour to the east.

Tampa

ADVENTURE ISLAND

This outdoor water theme park has slides and tubes, a wave pool, a swimming and diving area and beautiful white sands.
4500 Bougainvillea Avenue. Tel: (813) 987–5660. Open: spring 10am–5pm, summer 9am–8pm. Admission charge.

Fun on the rapids at Busch Gardens

BUSCH GARDENS

The most visited theme park in Florida after Walt Disney World, Busch Gardens' eight theme areas include a Congo section, a Moroccan marketplace, tropical Bird Gardens and Timbuktu. You could be in the veldt watching zebras and other animals, or touring the Serengeti by monorail (see page 37).
Busch Boulevard and 40th Street. Tel: (813) 987–5082. Open: 9.30am–6pm (check summer). Admission charge.

HARBOUR ISLAND

This festive waterfront complex just south of Tampa's business district has colourful entertainment, good speciality shops and a choice of restaurants. You can take to the water on a paddleboat or board a 70-year-old Venetian gondola.
601 South Harbour Island Boulevard. Tel: (813) 229–5093. Shops open: Monday to Saturday 10am–9pm, Sunday noon–5pm.

HENRY B PLANT MUSEUM

Plant's old hotel is his memorial and is now part of the university and a National Historic Landmark. Displays include original hotel furnishings, Wedgwood pottery and Oriental art (see page 36).
401 West Kennedy Boulevard. Tel: (813) 254–1891. Open: Tuesday to Saturday 10am–4pm, Sunday noon–4pm. Admission charge.

LOWRY PARK ZOO

This recently renovated zoo has shaded boardwalks winding through natural habitats which include Primate World, the Asian Domain and a Manatee and Aquatic Center. Adjacent to the zoo is Lowry Amusement Park, a favourite with children (see page 37).
7530, North Boulevard. Tel: (813) 935–0245. Guided tours. Open: autumn to winter 9.30am–5pm, spring to summer 9.30am–6pm. Admission charge.

The modern Museum of Art at Tampa with its fine collection of antiquities

MUSEUM OF SCIENCE AND INDUSTRY (MOSI)

Florida's largest science centre features hands-on displays including a simulated hurricane, a space-shuttle mission and a Wizard's Workshop. The Back Woods offers three trails to explore through a 40-acre wilderness (see page 37).

4801 East Fowler Street. Tel: (813) 987–6300. Open: Sunday to Thursday 9am–6pm, Friday and Saturday 9am–9pm. Admission charge.

TAMPA BAY PERFORMING ARTS CENTER

This six-year-old triple theatre complex is Tampa's cultural pride and joy. It is one of the largest cultural centres in the South, with music and events of all kinds, to suit all tastes.

1010 North MacInnes Plaza. Information – Box Office tel: (813) 221–1045.

TAMPA MUSEUM OF ART

The seven galleries here hold changing exhibitions as well as permanent collections of Egyptian, Greek and Roman antiquities. There are also lectures, hands-on activities and films.

601 Doyle Carlton Drive. Tel: (813) 223–8130. Tours. Open: Tuesday to Saturday 10am–5pm, Wednesday 10am–9pm, Sunday 1–5pm.

YBOR CITY STATE MUSEUM AND PRESERVATION PARK

In a former bakery, Ybor City State Museum contains *memorabilia* and photographs from the old cigar industry of the 19th century. The park next door has six renovated, turn-of-the-century cigar workers' homes and 'La Casita', an old 'shotgun' house furnished in typical 1895 style (see page 37).

Museum: 1818 9th Avenue. Information tel: (813) 247–6323. Open: Tuesday to Saturday 9am–noon, 1–5pm. Small admission charge.

Huge turn-of-the-century brick warehouses occupy Ybor Square

YBOR SQUARE

Ornate grills and blown-glass windows set the mood with the former V M Ybor Cigar Factory reflecting the city's Cuban past. Hand-rolled cigars are on display and there are speciality stores and ethnic restaurants in the old warehouse (see page 37).

1901 N 13th Street. Tel: (813) 247–4497. Shops open: Monday to Saturday 9.30am–5.30pm, Sunday noon–5.30pm.

FRESHWATER FLORIDA

They say that wherever you are in Florida the sea is never more than 60 miles away. The nearest fresh water, however, is likely to be considerably closer. Rivers, lakes and springs occur so frequently that it sometimes seems that Florida has more water than land, a freshwater wilderness surrounded by limitless sea.

At springs such as Homosassa in the west, an underwater observatory brings you face-to-face with manatees, and at Falling Waters, near Chipley in the north, a 67-foot waterfall plunges down a 100-foot sinkhole to unknown depths underground.

Nobody has yet counted all the lakes, but there are at least 20 which are significantly large. Lake Okeechobee, the 'hole' in the centre

The deep water springs at Homosassa form a natural aquarium where water creatures can be closely observed

of a Florida map, at 700 square miles, is the second largest American freshwater lake entirely within the United States.

With the lakes, Florida's main rivers, such as the Suwannee, St John's, Loxahatchee and more, plus their tributaries, are also popular for swimming, fishing and boating. Many also have springs, such as Blue Springs, with its manatees, on the St John's. Wekiwa Springs, on the tributary of the river of the same name, has a 19-mile canoe route.

Most of Central Florida's waters drain south into Lake Okeechobee, spilling over into the Everglades where the 6-inch-deep, 50-mile-wide River of Grass moves imperceptibly south. A fine canoe trail, the Wilderness Waterway, runs north from Flamingo through the untouched west some 100 miles to Everglades City.

Until recently, people believed that Florida's waters were unlimited, but now the state knows better. Areas of marsh, swamp and other wetlands, cleared in less ecologically aware times, are being reinstated and new environmental regulations are strict. This is not only to the benefit of the residents, but also for those who come to Florida for the delight of being beside or on the waters.

Boating on the Suwannee River. Hiking, camping and fishing can all be enjoyed along its banks too

The North

*T*o the European visitor, the north of Florida is largely unknown territory. To American visitors, it's the bit they hit first on their headlong winter drive south, their first opportunity to thaw northern bones and soak up the sun. The North holds the state capital, Tallahassee, and is the only part of Florida that has something of the atmosphere of a traditional Southern State.

Early settlers

The first European arrived in the north of Florida in 1513, when Ponce de León landed near St Augustine. He did not stay, however, and it was not until 1565, that St Augustine became what is claimed to be the first permanent settlement in North America.

Six years earlier, another conquistador, Tristan de Luna, had already established a colony of some 1,500 people on the shores of Pensacola Bay, in the west. The early settlement of Pensacola was destroyed in a devastating storm, leaving St Augustine as the oldest settlement in the state.

The 27th State

Florida became a state as late as 1845, and because Tallahassee was a natural mid-way point between the early important colonial cities of St Augustine

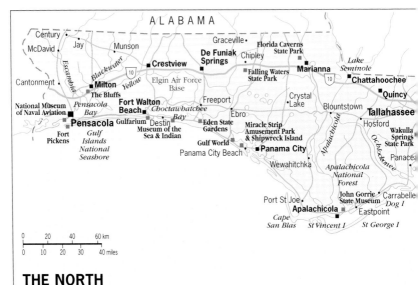

THE NORTH

and Pensacola, it was chosen as the state capital. It is set in countryside that few associate with Florida: rolling hills and plantations, crossed by canopy roads, where the trees meet overhead.

Across the Panhandle

If peninsular Florida is the pan, then the long thin strip of northern Florida bordering Georgia and Alabama is the panhandle. Interstate 10 is the link that joins east to west. It runs from the commercial hub of Jacksonville, threading its way through Osceola National Forest (named after the last Seminole chief), in and out of Tallahassee, then on through half a dozen state parks, across Escambia Bay, where the nearby city of Milton is a reminder that the rivers and bays once meant trade and shipping, and on to the historic city of Pensacola. The I–10

heads out of the State west into Alabama.

In January and February it seems as if the Florida 'panhandle' has more visitors from the cold Northern states than Florida residents. In summer, the Southerners of Alabama and Georgia come to their summer homes along the Florida coastline for respite from the stifling heat.

The Emerald Coast

US 98 runs alongside the sugar-white sands and green waters of the Gulf of Mexico and over a multitude of inter-connecting bridges. The road connects Pensacola Beach, Fort Walton Beach, Destin, the beaches of South Walton, Panama City Beach and Panama City. Head south of Wakulla Springs and Tallahassee until the road rejoins peninsular Florida.

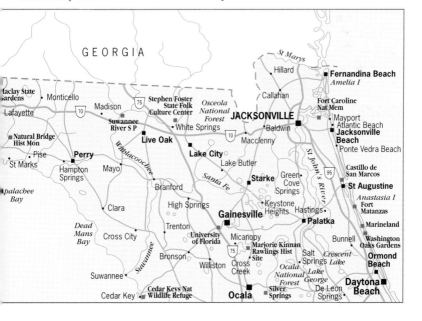

The Northeast – St Augustine

*P*edro Menéndez de Avilés, who founded St Augustine in 1565, would be heartened to know that those who came after him did not tear it down and start again. The 17th-century Castillo de San Marcos still guards the town and its water approaches. The oldest house goes back to the early 1600s, and the restored Spanish Quarter to the 1740s. Many streets are pedestrianised – fortunately, because the only real way to explore St Augustine is on foot.

St Augustine is the county seat of St John's County, at the heart of nearly 50 miles of beach stretching from Ponte Vedra in the north to Fort Matanzas in the south. St Augustine Beach is on Anastasia Island, divided from the town by the Intracoastal Waterway.

CASTILLO DE SAN MARCOS

Before the stone Castillo, St Augustine had nine wooden forts, the last of which was burned down by Sir Francis Drake in 1568. The present huge square fortress was built from coquina, a mixture of shell and cement, by the Spanish between 1672 and 1695. Its moat and outer defences are still in stout condition, despite many concerted attacks. The most famous assault culminated in a 27-day siege, when townspeople and soldiers crammed into the fort, until too much sun, too many insects and too little water forced the attacking British to withdraw.

The Castillo has never been taken by force of arms, but in 1763 it surrendered into British hands, when Spain exchanged Florida for Havana, which had just been captured by the British. A climb to the top of the ramparts is rewarded with a fine view of the area and the Matanzas river (see page 22).
1 Castillo Drive East. Tel: (904)

The impregnable Castillo de San Marcos

829–6506. *Guided tours. Open:*
9am–5.15pm, summer 9am–6pm.
Admission charge.

CROSS AND SWORD

This is Florida's official state play, by
Pulitzer Prize-winner, Paul Green. A
cast of 50 actors, dancers and musicians
relive early Spanish colonial history on a
110-foot outdoor stage in Anastasia
Island State Park.
St Augustine Amphitheatre, Highway A1A
South. Times and bookings: tel: (904)
471–1965. Open: mid-June to end-August.
Nightly (except Sunday). Admission charge.

FORT MATANZAS

Reached by free ferry some 14 miles
south on A1A South, this southern
watchtower of the Castillo de San
Marcos overlooks the Intracoastal
Waterway.
    It was never conquered but fell into
disuse after 1821. It is surrounded by a
beautiful 290-acre park with a good
swimming beach and ferry dock.
A1A South. Tel: (904) 471–0116. Ferry
(summer) 9am–4.30pm from tip of island
opposite. Open: 8.30am–5.30pm. Closed:
Christmas Day.

LEGENDARY FOUNTAIN OF YOUTH

This is reported to be the spot where
Ponce de León first set foot on Florida
soil in 1513, possibly searching for the
fabled Fountain of Youth, but more
likely in search of gold. An ancient
spring does flow here, however, and
therefore maintains the legend. The
surrounding gardens and archaeological
park contain a planetarium, a cross of
coquina stones, first excavated in the
mid-19th century, excavations of a
2,000-year-old Timucuan Indian

BLOODSHED ON THE BAY

Matanzas, as in Matanzas Bay and
Fort Matanzas, is Spanish for
slaughter and refers to one of the
darkest episodes in the history of this
coast. In 1565 some 200 to 300
unarmed French Huguenots were
massacred by the forces of Menéndez
where Fort Matanzas now stands, in
retaliation for a failed French attack.
The Spanish Catholic forces
perceived the Protestant newcomers
not only as territorial invaders but
also as religious heretics, and
therefore had few qualms about
putting them to the sword.

---

settlement, and the first Christian Indian
burial ground in North America.
155 Magnolia Avenue. Tel: (904)
829–3168. Open: 9am–5pm. Admission
charge.

LIGHTHOUSE MUSEUM

This black and white-striped landmark
was built in 1871 to warn against the
main inlet's dreaded shifting sands. You
can climb to the top for a fine view of the
bay and town. The newly restored
Lighthouse Keeper's House is now a
coastal museum.
81 Lighthouse Avenue (opposite Alligator
Farm). Tel: (904) 829–0745. Open:
10am–5pm. Admission charge.

LIGHTNER ANTIQUE HALL

Below the Lightner Museum the former
indoor swimming pool can be visited
(reached by a side entrance). The
Alcazar Café is at the 'deep end', and
there are two galleries of antique shops.
Concerts are sometimes held here.
Granada Street. Open: 10am–5pm.

LIGHTNER MUSEUM

The personal collection of businessman Otto C Lightner is one of Florida's finest exhibitions of antiques, collectables, mechanical instruments and Victorian bric-à-brac, housed in the splendid 1888 Alcazar Hotel. Notice the Tiffany glass above the doorways and the magnificent doll's house (see page 22).

75 King Street. Tel: (904) 824–2874. Guided tours. Open: 9am–5pm. Closed: Christmas Day. Admission charge.

MARINELAND OF FLORIDA

This fine marine-life park, claimed to be the oldest in the world, features performing dolphins, underwater hand-feeding of sharks, barracuda and stingrays, and a 3-D film, *Sea Dream,* where monsters of the deep seem to come right out of the screen.

9507 Ocean Shore Boulevard (16 miles south on A1A south, not far from Fort Matanzas). Tel: (904) 471–1111. Guided tours (on request). Open: daily 9am–5.30pm.

THE OLDEST DRUG STORE

A real old apothecary's shop, with talking wax figures behind the counter, a selection of old-time potions in glass jars, an 1843 cash register and many original 18th- and 19th-century fittings.

Corner of Cordova Street and Orange Street. Open during shop hours.

THE OLDEST HOUSE

The site of the González-Alvarez House has been continuously occupied since the early 1600s. The house is furnished to reflect its different periods and contains many historical reminders, such as the Historical Society's Research Library, the Manucy Museum of St Augustine History, and Florida's Army

Museum (see page 23).

14 St Francis Street. Tel: (904) 824–2872. Guided tours. Open: 9am–5pm. Admission charge.

The Fernandez-Llambias House (no 31 St Francis Street), is typical of St Augustine's heritage (see page 22). Pre-1763, it was a single-storey house. A British owner added a gallery; Minorcan settlers gave it a second storey and, from 1854 to 1919, Dona Catalina Llambias turned it into a family house.

THE OLDEST STORE MUSEUM

Take another look into yesteryear in this old general store, where around 100,000 original stock items range from starched collars and red flannel underwear to penny-farthing bicycles.

4 Artillery Lane. Tel: (904) 829–9729. Guided tours. Open: Monday to Saturday 9am–5pm, Sunday noon–5pm. Admission charge.

THE OLD JAIL

This grim place functioned as St John's County Jail from 1891 to 1953. The jokey courtyard display of felons in black and white hooped prison suits contrasts with the depressing crumbling cell blocks and the collection of guns and other criminal weapons.

167 San Marco Avenue. Tel: (904) 824–2872. Open: 8.30am–5pm.

THE OLD SCHOOLHOUSE

This atmospheric cedar- and cypress-boarded building is held together by wooden pegs and hand-made nails. It was built some time before 1763 and is thought to be the country's oldest schoolhouse. You can see a 'class' in session and press a button to hear a schoolroom soundtrack. One old photograph of the class of 1864 shows

the last surviving pupil, who lived to
1944.
14 St George Street. Tel: (904) 824–0192.
Open: 9am–5pm (summer to 7pm).
Admission charge.

ST AUGUSTINE ALLIGATOR FARM

A boardwalk runs over an alligator
swamp and there are alligator and reptile
shows. The star of the farm, however, is
the New Guinea saltwater crocodile,
Gomek, at 17 feet 5 inches and 1,750
pounds, the world's largest crocodile.
*A1A South (over bridge to Anastasia
Island). Tel: (904) 824–3337. Open:
9am–5pm. Admission charge.*

ST AUGUSTINE TOURS

There are several guided tours on offer:
trolley, train, horse and carriage, boat, or
on foot.

For information and bookings
contact the following:
Historical Tours:
Tel: (904) 829–3800.
Sightseeing Trains:
Tel: (904) 829–6545.

Safer than swamps for alligator-watching

St Augustine's ancient wooden school

Colee's Carriage Tours:
Tel: (904) 829–2818.
Victory II & III Scenic Cruise:
Tel: (904) 824–1806.
Tours by Mary Way Jacobs:
Walking and other guided tours.
Tel: (904) 829–5598.

ZORAYDA CASTLE

Built by millionaire Franklin Smith in
1883, this is a replica of a wing of the
12th-century Alhambra in Granada,
reflecting the life and entertainments of
the old Moorish rulers of southern Spain
in a palm-studded setting.
83 King Street. Tel: (904) 824–3097.
Guided tours. Open: 9am–5.30pm.
Admission charge.

HISPANIC FLORIDA

Great Cross, where the Spanish first landed

Florida has six districts which print their ballot papers in Spanish as well as English, four in the south, the other two in the west around Tampa.

Hispanic influence has been a fact of Florida life from Ponce de León's landing in 1513, and Hernando de Soto's explorations a decade or two later. They were followed by settlers, and much of Florida, at least in name, was Spanish for nearly 200 years. Then,

the bewildered Floridians found themselves briefly British, then Spanish once more until 1821, when Florida became American.

Spain lives on in both St Augustine and Pensacola in surnames, place names and memory. The former's Spanish Quarter is part of the authentic city of 1740, and Pensacola's Seville Historic District goes back to the same century.

Hispanic culture of later times is

The Spanish Quarter,
St Augustine

Flamenco dancing
in the streets at
festival time

Muskets being ceremoniously
fired in Spanish military dress

best seen in Ybor City, part of
Tampa, named after Vicente
Martínez Ybor, one of three cigar
manufacturers who successfully
lured the Cuban cigar industry from
Key West. The Cubans in turn
attracted other Hispanics, and
today the influence shows in the
whole *café con leche* tempo of life.

So close to Cuba, the Keys' links
are strong with Hispanic culture,
both past and present, but Miami
has the greatest modern

involvement.

The best time to taste the
flavour of a Spanish influence that
has lasted more than 400 years is at
festival times. From Holy Week
with its Passion Play and Christmas
parades in St Augustine to the
Latin-style Halloween festivities of
Ybor City, and the great annual
Miami Carnaval, culminating in
Calle Ocho, Hispanic tradition is
still a strong part of Florida today.

The Northeast – Jacksonville

*T*he cosmopolitan, commercial city of Jacksonville has always had a close affinity with the St John's River. Its riverboat trade may have slowed in recent years but the city has used its most vital asset as the site for a downtown shopping and restaurant complex on the north bank and a boardwalk on the south bank, pumping life and energy back into the riverfront. Though it is the north's main commercial hub, Jacksonville is less than a half-hour car ride to long beaches for surfing, swimming and deep-sea fishing.

Twenty-five miles north, Amelia Island has one of the coast's best barrier island beaches and the only town, Fernandina Beach, features 50 blocks of Victorian architecture, listed on the US National Register of Historic Places.

AMELIA ISLAND MUSEUM OF HISTORY

Amelia Island has lived under eight flags since 1562 (French, Spanish, British, Patriots, Green Cross of Florida, Mexican, Confederate and American), so this small museum has no shortage of colourful historical tales or exhibits, some from digs at the Spanish mission site. Guided walking tours of Fernandina's historic district leave from here.
233 South 3rd Street, Fernandina Beach. Tel: (904) 261-7378. Open: 11am–2pm. Admission charge.

AMERICAN LIGHTHOUSE MUSEUM

Scale models and hundreds of old photographs and navigational aids explain the historical role of American lighthouses in this small museum.
1911 N Third Street, Jacksonville Beach. Tel: (904) 241-8845. Open: Tuesday to Saturday 10am-5pm.

The futuristic skyline of downtown Jacksonville City beyond St John's River. Main Street Bridge links the north and south banks

ANHEUSER-BUSCH BREWERY TOUR

Find out how they make Budweiser and many other beers at this huge brewery, which offers tours and samplings.
111 Busch Drive, Jacksonville. Tel: (904) 751–8116. Open: Monday to Saturday, winter 9am–4pm, summer to 5pm.

CENTRE STREET, FERNANDINA BEACH

This is the main street of the picturesque historic town of Fernandina Beach. Most of the buildings here are shops, superbly restored to their original Victorian condition. Call at the Chamber of Commerce, which occupies the old railroad depot by the shrimp docks, for general information. Guided tours of the Historic District on and around Centre Street start from Amelia Island Museum of History and include some interiors of private houses. In May, the annual shrimp festival features arts, crafts and antiques, a 'pirate invasion', the Blessing of the Fleet and shrimping demonstrations.
Chamber of Commerce, 102 Centre Street (A1A). Tel: (904) 277–0171. Open: normal shopping hours.

CUMMER GALLERY OF ART

Beautiful waterfront gardens surround this outstanding fine arts museum and cultural centre which specialises in 17th-century Dutch and Flemish paintings, and Chinese and Meissen porcelain. A permanent collection of over 2,000 items is complemented by changing exhibitions.
829 Riverside Avenue, Jacksonville. Tel: (904) 356–6857. Guided tours (in advance). Open: Tuesday to Friday 10am–4pm, Saturday noon–5pm, Sunday 2–5pm.

FORT CAROLINE NATIONAL MEMORIAL

Florida's first Protestant colony was settled by French Huguenots here in 1564. Today a replica fort overlooks the St John's River. There is a museum, nature trails and, adjacent, the Theodore Roosevelt Wildlife Preserve covers a beautiful natural area.
12713 Fort Caroline Road, Jacksonville. Tel: (904) 641–7155. Guided tours. Open: 9am–5pm.

FORT CLINCH STATE PARK

Built in 1847 and occupied by both sides during the American Civil War, Fort Clinch is in an outstanding state of repair. A small 'garrison of Civil War soldiers' escorts visitors on a tour of the fort. On the first weekend each month they re-enact Civil War episodes (see page 41).
2601 Atlantic Avenue, Fernandina Beach. Tel: (904) 261–4212. Guided tours. Open: 8am to sunset.

JACKSONVILLE ART MUSEUM

The city's oldest museum has everything from pre-Columbian artefacts to contemporary painting and sculpture. The collection of Chinese porcelain is one of the highlights.
4160 Boulevard Center Drive, Jacksonville. Tel: (904) 398–8336. Guided tours. Open: Tuesday to Friday 10am–4pm, Thursday to 10pm, Saturday and Sunday 1–5pm.

JACKSONVILLE LANDING

This attractive riverside shopping complex has restaurants, dozens of speciality shops and an international food hall all under one roof, with music, drama, fireworks and mime shows.
2 Independent Drive, Jacksonville. Tel: (904) 353–1188.

JACKSONVILLE ZOOLOGICAL PARK

More than 800 birds, reptiles and mammals make their home in this 62-acre park, one of the oldest and most famous attractions in the city. Other features include Okavango Village for children, and the Okavango Trail and Landing, based on the African veldt.
8605 Zoo Road, Jacksonville. Tel: (904) 757–4463. Open: 9am–5pm. Closed: Christmas and New Year's Days and Thanksgiving. Admission charge.

KINGSLEY PLANTATION SITE

Dating from 1792, Florida's oldest existing plantation was once owned by a slave trader. It is now a State Historic Site on Fort George Island. Enthusiastic rangers will tell you about the conditions the slaves lived and worked in. You can tour the main house which was built in 1817 (see page 41).
11676 Palmetto Avenue. Tel: (904) 251–3122. Guided tours. Open: 8am–5pm. Admission charge.

MAYPORT AND ITS FERRY

A drive northeast across the ferry to Mayport takes you to one of the oldest American fishing communities (see page 41). Now it has a large commercial shrimping fleet. The nostalgic car ferry plies its way across the St John's between Mayport and Fort George Island (for Kingsley Plantation).
Ferry open: 6.20am–10.15pm. Charge.

MAYPORT NAVAL STATION

The home of the USS *Saratoga*, this is one of the largest naval bases in America, and the busiest in Florida. It is home to cruisers, frigates, destroyers, mine-sweepers and aircraft carriers (see page 41).

1347 Palmer Street, Mayport. Tel: (904) 241–NAVY. Public tours of visiting ships on Saturdays and Sundays. Open (for tours): Saturday 10am–4.30pm, Sunday 1–4.30pm.

METROPOLITAN PARK

Overlooking the river, this lovely 23-acre grassy park on the north side of the river is a popular outdoor music venue. The St John's River City Band regularly plays jazz and folk. River Fest and Country Music Fest are staged in April, and the Spring Music Fest happens in May. Each October the largest free jazz festival in the country is held here.
North Bank, Jacksonville. Tel: (904) 630–0837 and 630–3520.

MUSEUM OF SCIENCE AND HISTORY

This 70,000-square-foot museum on three floors has scientific, historical and anthropological exhibits, including many hands-on activities, a large planetarium and a marine aquarium.
1025 Gulf Life Drive, Jacksonville. Tel: (904) 396–7062. Open: Monday to Thursday 10am–5pm, Friday and Saturday 10am–6pm, Sunday 1–6pm. Admission charge.

The Museum of Science and History

The University of Florida Art Gallery at Gainesville

THE RIVERWALK

The mile-plus stroll along this old-fashioned boardwalk is lined with hotels, restaurants, food vendors and entertainment. Many special events are held here, including an arts and crafts festival in May.
851 N Market Street, Jacksonville. Tel: (904) 396-4900. Open: regular shopping hours.

GAINESVILLE

This old town is 85 miles southwest od Jacksonville.

FLORIDA MUSEUM OF NATURAL HISTORY

Florida's largest museum of natural history features a replica of a prehistoric limestone cave, fossils, skeletons, a Mayan temple and a typical Timucuan Indian household.
Museum Road/Newell Drive. Tel: (904) 392-1721. Open: Monday to Saturday 10am–4pm, Sunday 1–4pm.

KANAPAHA BOTANICAL GARDENS

Relax in delightful woodlands and meadows with herbs, butterflies and the largest collection of bamboo in Florida.
4625 SW 63rd Boulevard. Tel: (904)

372–4981. Open: Monday, Tuesday and Friday 9am–5pm, Wednesday, Saturday and Sunday till dusk. Closed: Thursdays. Admission charge.

MARJORIE KINNAN RAWLINGS HISTORIC SITE

Set deep in the heart of unspoiled Florida countryside, this is the home of Marjorie Kinnan Rawlings, awarded the 1939 Pulitzer prize for her novel *The Yearling*.
Cross Creek, 21 miles southeast of Gainesville on Highway 325. Open: Thursday to Monday 10am–11.30am, 1–4.30pm. Closed: Tuesday and Wednesday. Admission charge.

Walkway through Jacksonville Zoo

UNIVERSITY OF FLORIDA HISTORIC CAMPUS

Wander through the elegant portals and pillars of buildings on the National Register of Historic Places, and see alligators on Lake Alice at the western end of Museum Road.
SW 13th Street (US 441), SW 2nd Avenue, Gainesville. Main entrance for passes.

Tallahassee and Northwest

TALLAHASSEE

It seems odd that such a small, quiet town so far removed from the hubbub of Central and Southern Florida should be the state capital. Tallahassee was given this honour back in 1824 simply because it lay halfway on the long, dangerous journey between the state's two principal towns, Pensacola and St Augustine. Despite the fact that half of the Florida population now lives south of Orlando, Tallahassee has still managed to retain its status.

Old-fashioned charm

Despite being a capital, Tallahassee has not become a traffic-clogged, urban jungle. On the contrary, it resembles more a well-kept, prosperous provincial centre with a harmonious blend of old and new and abundant greenery. Only 14 miles from Georgia, it has Southern charm and a blend of government, academic and artistic influences.

CANOPY ROADS

Walk or drive down some of these roads where moss-draped live oak form lovely arcades. Five in Tallahassee are specially protected. They are St Augustine, Miccosukee, Meridian, Old Bainbridge and Centerville roads.

CAPITOL COMPLEX

The best way to get a feel of modern-day Tallahassee is from the 22nd-floor observation gallery of the New Capitol. Views sweep out over the city, its plantations, and (on a clear day) as far as the Gulf of Mexico. Down below, you can visit the Old Capitol, and (Monday to Friday only) the Secretary of State's reception room, and the Cabinet meeting room.
Adams Street/Monroe Street. Tel: (904) 487–1902. Guided tours: Monday to Friday 9am–4pm, Saturday and Sunday 11am–3pm.

DE SOTO HISTORIC SITE

Here, the Spanish expedition leader Hernando de Soto camped and celebrated Christmas for the first time in

A '30s house and car on the De Soto Site

North America in 1539. Archaeologists discovered the site in 1986 and have dug out the oldest copper coins in America. It is also the site of a 1930s-era home built for Florida Governor John Martin; it is now being restored.
Corner of Lafayette Street and Goodbody Lane. Tel: (904) 488–7588 for opening times.

THE 1840 HOUSE, MARIANNA

A glimpse into Victorian domestic life with architecture, furnishings and antiques from many periods.
244 Lafayette Street, Marianna, 65 miles northwest of Tallahassee. Tel: (904) 482–5624. Open: Monday to Saturday 10am–5pm, Sunday 1–5pm.

FLORIDA CAVERNS STATE PARK

The extensive connecting limestone caverns here have some spectacular stalactite and stalagmite formations. The largest and most impressive caves are lit and open to the public for ranger-guided tours. The park also offers facilities for swimming, a horse trail and canoe rentals.
2701 Caverns Road, Marianna. Tel: (904) 482–9598. Guided tours. Open: 9am–4pm. Admission charge.

KNOTT HOUSE MUSEUM

This 1843 house holds a lot of state history. Built by a free black builder, it saw the first emancipation of North Florida slaves in 1865, became the laboratory for Florida's first black physician, and home to Supreme Court judges and many political figures.
301 E Park Avenue, Tallahassee. Tel: (904) 922–2459. Open: 10am–4pm daily. Handicapped facilities. Guided tours. Admission charge.

A charming contrived view in the Maclay ornamental gardens

MACLAY STATE GARDENS

After her husband's death, the widow of New York financier Alfred B Maclay took on his dream of creating an outstanding ornamental garden. The star blooms are the 100 varieties of camellias and the 50 kinds of azaleas, but another 160 exotic species complement these. The season is from January to April with the peak time being mid- to late March. The adjacent park also offers picnics, swimming, boating and nature study.
3450 Thomasville Road, 5 miles northeast of Tallahassee on US 319. Tel: (904) 487–4556. For guided tours of garden and house telephone in advance. Open: 8am–sunset. Admission charge.

MONTICELLO HISTORIC DISTRICT

This 27-block historic district is best seen on foot, though you can drive. The old opera house now produces mainly regional theatre with a Southern flavour.
Highway 90, 26 miles northeast of Tallahassee. Monticello-Jefferson Chamber of Commerce, 420 W Washington Street. For information tel: (904) 997–5552. Opera House: tel: (904) 997–4242.

MUSEUM OF FLORIDA HISTORY

This well-designed, interesting, modern museum traces the history of Florida from prehistoric times and includes such large-scale exhibits as 'Herman', the 9-foot-tall mastodon, pulled from Wakulla Springs in 1930s, and a reconstructed steamboat section.
R A Gray Building, 500 S Bronough Street. Tel: (904) 488–1484. Open: Monday to Friday 10am–4.30pm, Saturday noon–4.30pm.

NATURAL BRIDGE BATTLEFIELD SITE

The Confederate victory here in 1865 meant that Tallahassee was the only Confederate capital not captured during the Civil War. There is a monument and

The Opera House in Monticello

an annual battle re-enactment.
13 miles southeast of Tallahassee (off SR 363). Tel: (904) 925–6216. Open: 8am–sunset.

ST MARK'S HISTORIC RAILROAD TRAIL

Once an important 19th-century railroad, the tracks are gone and this 16-mile trail to St Mark's now carries hikers, horse riders and cyclists.
Car park on SR 363 south of the city at Tallahassee/St Mark's Railroad Trail. Tel: (904) 925–6216.

WAKULLA SPRINGS STATE PARK

Wakulla claims one of the world's largest and deepest freshwater springs. Glass-bottom boat rides allow visitors to see down to the entrance of the spring cavern some 100 feet below. Several early Tarzan movies were filmed here, also *The Creature from the Black Lagoon*.
1 Springs Drive, Wakulla Springs, 14 miles south of Tallahassee on SR 267. Tel: (904) 222–7279. Guided tours. Open: 8am–sunset. Admission charge waived if you dine in the restaurant.

In and Around Pensacola and the Emerald Coast

Six years before his countrymen were to found St Augustine in 1565, Don Tristan de Luna settled a colony of some 1,500 people on Pensacola Bay. Had it not been for a devastating hurricane soon after then, Pensacola would today be acclaimed as the oldest city in Florida. As it was, de Luna abandoned Pensacola and it was not rediscovered for almost another 200 years.

Today, Pensacola is a modern city, a thriving port and the home of the US Naval Air Service. A rich history and a mixture of nationalities – American Indian, Spanish, Scottish, French, English, Creole – have left three historic districts with numerous fascinating buildings.

THE CIVIL WAR SOLDIERS' MUSEUM

See the war in full-size dioramas of a Union camp and a confederate field hospital. Push a button and hear a soldier's letter home, or read diaries from Fort Pickens. There are also uniforms, weapons and relics of Florida's involvement in the conflict.
108 South Palafox Place. Tel: (904) 469–1900. Guided tours. Open: Monday to Saturday 10am–4.30pm. Admission charge.

HISTORIC DISTRICTS

Pensacola has three districts: Seville, based on Seville Square and the Bay Front, where the survivors of a hurricane on Santa Rosa settled in 1752; Palafox, the old commercial centre; and North Hill, a high-class residential area created between 1870 and the 1930s. The Historic Pensacola Village is a grouping of various types of museums devoted to West Florida history.
205 E Zaragoza Street. Tel: (904) 444–8905. Open: 10am–4pm. Closed: Sunday. Admission charge.

Hoping for a catch off Pensacola Beach – the white sands stretching along the southern side of Santa Rosa Island. The town, to the east, is packed with historic buildings

NATIONAL MUSEUM OF NAVAL AVIATION

This outstanding museum relates the history of aviation from the dawn of flight to space exploration, in the home of the Blue Angels air display team. Allow plenty of time to view one of the country's largest and finest historic collections of Navy, Marine Corps and Coast Guard air-craft including the NC-4 Flying Boat and the F6F Hellcat. You can take the controls in the simulators which are situated around the museum.
Naval Air Station, (SR 295 South). Tel: Freephone (904) 453–NAVY. Guided tours. Open: 9am–5pm.

THE SCENIC HIGHWAY AND BAY BLUFFS

For an unusual view of Escambia Bay, take Highway 90 northeast out of Pensacola. At the junction of Scenic Highway and Summit Boulevard, an elevated boardwalk runs along the towering bluffs above the bay. The Bay Bluffs, unique in Florida, were formed by a prehistoric cataclysm. The best time to visit is during daylight hours. No ramp is available for disabled people.
Pensacola Department of Leisure Service for information. Tel: (904) 435–1770.

T T WENTWORTH JR FLORIDA STATE MUSEUM

A handsomely restored Mediterranean-Revival-style building of 1908, which was once City Hall, now holds many unexpected objects and *memorabilia* relating to the archaeology and history of West Florida.
330 S Jefferson Street. Tel: (904) 444–8586. Guided tours. Open: Monday to Saturday, winter and fall 10am–4pm, spring and summer 10am–4.30, Sunday 1–4pm. Admission charge.

THE EMERALD COAST

White sand beaches stretch 100 miles along the Gulf of Mexico, from Pensacola Beach to Panama City and beyond. Sea oats wave gently on the bright white dunes while emerald waters lap the foreshore. At evening the sky is an ever-changing palette of the reds, purples and yellows of a Gulf sunset. Along this coast of bays, channels and islands are more than a dozen state parks and numerous small communities, each with its own character and attractions.

AIR FORCE ARMAMENT MUSEUM

You'll find a hi-tech 'Blackbird' Spy plane and an enormous F-105 Thunderchief among the vintage aircraft, guns, rockets and missiles which have been part of the Air Force armament since World War I. Displays also include aerial armaments from both World Wars and the Korean and Vietnam Wars.
Eglin Air Force Base, SR 85, 6 miles northeast of Fort Walton Beach. Tel: (904) 882–4062. Open: 9.30am–4.30pm.

CONSTITUTIONAL CONVENTION STATE MUSEUM

St Joseph was an 1830s boom town built to compete with the port of Apalachicola, only to die in nine years after a yellow fever plague and a hurricane. The museum commemorates the town's high point as the place where Florida's first State Constitutional Convention drew up a formal application to join the Union.
200 Allen Memorial Way, Port St Joe (off US 98, 30 miles east of Panama City). Tel: (904) 229–8029. Open: 9am–noon, 1–5pm. Admission charge.

Fine naval aircraft can be seen at the National Museum of Aviation at Pensacola

EDEN STATE GARDENS

Once owned by a wealthy timber family, the restored late-19th-century Greek Revival-style mansion here overlooks Choctawhatchee Bay. Room furniture dates as far back as the 17th century. The gardens are best visited in March when the azaleas and dogwoods are in full bloom.

Point Washington, north of Highway 98, CR 395, S Walton. Tel: (904) 231–4214. Guided tours. Open: 8am–sunset. Closed: Tuesday and Wednesday. Admission charge.

FALLING WATERS STATE RECREATION AREA

The highlight of this park is a 67-foot waterfall which empties into a 100-foot-deep sinkhole, which can be seen from a vantage point above. The water then leaves the sinkhole via an underground river and caverns.

Off CR 276, 3 miles south of Chipley (30 miles north of Panama City Beach). Tel: (904) 638–4030. Open: 8am–sunset. Admission charge.

FORT PICKENS

The fort was completed by 400 slaves between 1829 and 1834 and ironically was held by Union forces in the Civil War. Later it became a prison for Indian Chief Geronimo.

West end of Santa Rosa Island (SR 399). Tel: (904) 932–5018. Guided tours. Open: 8am–sunset. Admission charge.

GULFARIUM

See dolphins, alligators, sea lions, seals, penguins, otters, and the Living Sea exhibit.

1010 Miracle Strip Parkway, Fort Walton Beach. Tel: (904) 244-5169. Open: autumn to spring 9am–4pm, summer 9am–6pm. Admission charge.

GULF BREEZE ZOO

From a Safari Line train you can see 600 animals, many free-roaming. Colossus, the world's largest captive gorilla, is a great favourite. Ride an elephant and feed a giraffe.

5701 Gulf Breeze Parkway (Highway 98). Tel: (904) 932–2229. Open: summer 9am–5pm, winter 9am–4pm. Admission charge.

GULF WORLD

Walk through tropical gardens and enjoy porpoise, sea lion and parrot shows plus scuba demonstrations and Penguin Island.

15412 Front Beach Road, Panama City Beach. Tel: (904) 234–5271. Open: autumn and winter 9am–5pm, spring and summer to 9pm. Admission charge.

INDIAN TEMPLE MOUND MUSEUM

The spiritual, artistic and technological achievements of seven pre-Columbian cultures indigenous to the Gulf Coast are displayed here.

2139 Miracle Strip Parkway, Fort Walton Beach. Tel: (904) 243–6521. Open: Monday to Saturday, September to May 11am–4pm, June to August 9am–4pm. Admission charge.

JOHN GORRIE STATE MUSEUM

Dr John Gorrie, a Scottish physician, came to the busy port of Apalachicola in the early 1800s. In an effort to cool the rooms of his fever patients, he invented the first ice-making machine, which was the forerunner of refrigeration and air conditioning. The original machine is now in the Smithsonian Institution, Washington DC, but you can see a replica here.

Gorrie Square, Apalachicola (historic district). Tel: (904) 653–9374. Open: 9am–noon, 1–5pm.

JUNIOR MUSEUM OF BAY COUNTY

See pioneer Florida with log cabins and early farming tools, go back to prehistoric times with the dinosaur exhibit and enjoy hands-on fun and discovery.

1731 Jenks Avenue, Panama City. Tel: (904) 769–6128. Open: Monday to Friday 9am–4.30pm, Saturday 9am–4pm.

MIRACLE STRIP AMUSEMENT PARK

A popular family park with dozens of rides, arcades, carousels and attractions, including one of the country's most terrifying roller-coaster rides.

12001 Front Beach Road, Panama City Beach. Tel: (904) 234–5810. Open: varies with season.

THE MUSEUM OF MAN IN THE SEA

The museum serves as an education centre for the Institute of Diving. Trace the advances in underwater exploration with exhibits ranging from a 19th-century air-supply pump and a 1913 German armoured diving suit to modern scuba technology and diving chambers.

17314 Back Beach Road (US 98), Panama City Beach. Tel: (904) 235–4101. Open: 9am–5pm. Admission charge.

Enjoying a break at Shipwreck Island

MUSEUM OF THE SEA AND INDIAN

Exhibits from the ocean and Indian artefacts from North and South America are displayed here. A small zoo features alligators, peacocks, pheasants, ducks and monkeys.

4801 Beach Highway, Destin. Tel: (904) 837–6625. Open: winter 9am–4pm, spring and autumn 8am–5pm, summer 8am–6pm.

SHIPWRECK ISLAND WATER PARK

A large water park with a giant wave pool, a white-water tube ride, a 35mph racing slide, a 1,600-foot Lazy River ride and several themed areas for sunbathing.

12001 Front Beach Road, Panama City Beach. Tel: (904) 234-0368. Open: March to Labour Day 10am–6pm.

SNAKE-A-TORIUM

See snake 'milking' demonstrations in the reptile park, with rattlesnakes, giant pythons, monkeys and alligators.

9008 W Highway 98A, Panama City Beach. Tel: (904) 234-3311. Open: autumn and winter 10am–4pm, spring 9am–5pm, summer 8am–7pm. Admission charge.

WHITE GOLD

The sands on the Emerald Coast are a dazzling white because they are 99 per cent pure quartz, unlike most beaches which include ground sea shells. The sand actually squeaks underfoot because all the grains are the same size and rub together.

The spiky sea oats are invaluable because their network of roots binds the dunes together and holds them in place. The flower tops accumulate windblown sand which in turn becomes dunes and also act as storm buffers.

Getting Away From it All

*I*t can be surprisingly easy to get away from the billboards, theme parks and neon lights of metropolitan Florida and find a natural world. For Florida, with its mixture of temperate and tropical, has some of the best natural areas in the US, many of them either a national or state park. The most famous is the Everglades, but there are many lesser-known places which are equally unspoiled.

CEDAR KEY, West Coast

Nowadays, Cedar Key is a sleepy Victorian fishing village, but in the 19th century it was an important port and a haven for blockade runners exporting lumber, cotton and food to Confederate states. Many commercial cargoes passed through here, before the ships grew too large for the port's shallow harbour. Today, it still has a busy fishing and docking pier, fish houses, gift shops and art galleries. Don't miss Cedar Key State Museum where the town's historic importance is well documented.

Nine miles east are Waccasassa Bay and Cedar Key Scrub State Preserves, mostly salt marsh dotted by wooded islands and tidal creeks. Many fish, shellfish and crabs breed here, which accounts for the numbers of osprey, pelicans, herons and other birds, as well as otters and raccoons. Look out for endangered species such as the manatee, even a black bear or two, and the huge shape of the bald eagle high above. Spring is the best time to visit, when rangers lead canoe tours.

Cedar Key, at western end of SR 24. State Museum, off SR 24 on Museum Road. Tel: (904) 543–5350. Waccasassa Bay/Cedar Key Scrubs, PO Box 187, Cedar Key. Tel: (904) 543–5567. On SR 24, 9 miles east of Cedar Key. Open: daily 8am–sunset.

DE SOTO NATIONAL MEMORIAL, Bradenton, Tampa Bay, West

This memorial park celebrates the arrival of the Spanish explorer Hernando de Soto who is supposed to have landed at this very spot in May 1539. His four-year-long, 600-man voyage of exploration took him first through what is now North Florida, then across the southeast of the US to discover the Mississippi River. From December through April, the guides wear period dress and demonstrate various 16th-century weapons and different methods of food preparation and storage which were used long before refrigeration was available. There is also a year-round half-mile nature trail and an historical film every hour.

On Tampa Bay, 5 miles west of Bradenton, on 75th Street NW. Tel: (813) 792–0458. Open: daily 8am–5.30pm. Admission charge.

FORT JEFFERSON, Dry Tortugas

Fort Jefferson is only reached by boat or seaplane from Key West some 70 miles east. But it is worth it once you get there, not just for the sport fishing, snorkelling, swimming and scuba diving, but for its bird and other wildlife, and, above all, the great fortress, the largest all-masonry fort in the Western world. At first sight, its red-stone walls, 50 feet high and 8 feet thick, are astonishing in their size. Built in 1856 to control the Florida Straits, it was never completed. It was guarded by over 140 cannons, yet it has never fired a shot in anger.

Today, there are displays and self-guided tours to explain a past full of pirates, sunken treasure and shipwrecks. Fort Jefferson is the centrepiece of the seven Dry Tortugas Islands, surrounded by shoals and the waters of the Gulf of Mexico.

Because it is remote, visitors need to carry food, water, first aid and any other requirements from the mainland. Watch out also for crumbling walls.

Address: Everglades National Park, PO Box 279, Homestead FL 33030. Tel: (305) 247–6211.

Information on flights, boats – Chambers of Commerce, Marathon, tel: (305) 743–5417; Key West, (305) 294–2587; Naples, tel: (813) 262–6141.

Bird tours: Florida Nature Tours, PO Box 5643, Winter Park, Fl. 32793–5643. Tel: (407) 273–4400.

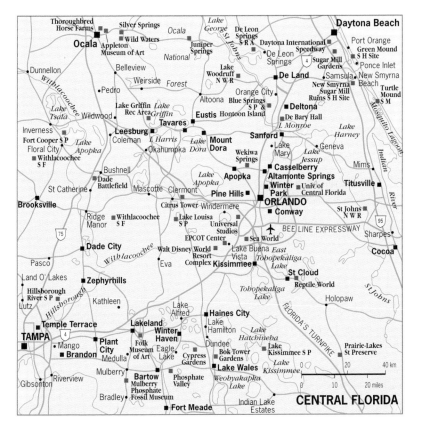

GULF ISLANDS NATIONAL SEASHORE,
Pensacola, North Florida

This huge conservation area is perfect for relaxation and recreation, with clear waters, gently sloping sands and a necklace of barrier islands and mainland bays. This is a historical area too, with ruined forts, and gun batteries to trace the past. There are historical tours, natural history tours, shrimp boats, and endless swimming, snorkelling and sailing.

1801 Gulf Breeze Parkway, Gulf Breeze. Tel: (904) 934–2600. From US 90, follow signs for Gulf Islands National Seashore. Open: daily 24 hours.

MYAKKA RIVER STATE PARK,
near Sarasota

This unspoiled 29,000-acre wildlife sanctuary is the biggest state park in Florida. In appearance it is similar to the Everglades in places, with grassy marshes and hammocks. There are over 37 miles of nature trails which you can

walk or bike along. Better still, take a Tram Safari during which you will travel off the main roads and learn about the region's flora and fauna. Alligators, deer, wild turkeys, foxes, bobcats and bald eagles are some of the animals you may spot. *Gator Gal* is the world's biggest airboat and is another enjoyable way of seeing the park.

14 miles east of Sarasota on SR72. Wildlife Tours, tel: (813) 365–0100. General park information, tel: (813) 924–1027.
Open: daily 8am–sunset. Admission charge.

PAYNES PRAIRIE AND CROSS CREEK, near Gainesville,
North Central Florida

When, in 1774, the plant collector and naturalist William Bartram described the 'great Alachua savannah', he was writing about the 18,000 acres of land which became Paynes Prairie, the largest cattle

You can boat, camp, hike, fish, swim or picnic in the 18,000-acre wildlife sanctuary of Paynes Prairie

ranch in Spanish Florida. In the 18th century, Seminole Indians moved here and their chief, King Payne, probably gave the area its name. The observation tower is good for watching waterfowl and wading birds, and visitors can fish, ride a horse, swim, picnic or walk.

A mile southwest is Micanopy, one of the oldest settlements in Florida. It has a charming main street with moss-draped live oaks, many historical buildings and is renowned for its antique shopping and annual antiques fair every autumn. Cross Creek was described by Marjorie Kinnan Rawlings as 'a bend in a country road by land and the flowing of Lochloosa Lake into Orange Lake by water'. She lived here and wrote about the local 'crackers' (original white rural settlers). Her Pulitzer prize-winning book, *The Yearling* was published in 1939. This rambling farmhouse was her home from 1928 to 1941, and she used it until her death in 1953. The 1890s house is a lovely unspoiled place, with frequent guided tours.

Marjorie Kinnan Rawlings Historic Site, 21 miles southeast of Gainesville on Highway 325. Tel: (904) 466–3672. Open: Thursday to Monday 10am–5pm. Closed: Tuesday and Wednesday. Admission charge.

WEKIWA SPRINGS STATE PARK, north of Orlando, Central Florida

It's hard to believe in this natural place that you are less than an hour from central Florida's man-made attractions. The springs are the headwater of the lush Wekiva River, which flows 15 miles into the St John's. The banks are quiet, under dense forest canopy, and full of birds and animals. Most people come for a day's river canoeing, or airboating and unless you specifically want to paddle

The American avocet's beak is specially adapted for feeding

upstream the best idea is to go to a river landing downstream. From here you can be transported up the river for 6, 10, 20 or more miles. You then paddle back gently down with the current. There's time to stop to swim or look at springs, old boats, an ancient Indian site, and the remains of an old railroad. It all makes for a wonderful day in the open.

1800 Wekiwa Circle, Apopka. Tel: (407) 889–9920. North from Orlando on I–4 East, turn left on to SR 436 (Junction 48), drive just over 3 miles and turn right on to N Wekiwa Springs Road for another mile. Open: daily 8am–sunset. Katie's Landing: 190 Katie's Cove, Sanford. Tel: (407) 628–1482. Drive north on I–4 East for about 16 miles from downtown Orlando. Turn left on to SR 46, follow it for 5 miles to exit right on to Wekiwa Park Drive, then 1 mile to Landing. Open: daily from 8am.

A BIRDWATCHER'S DREAM

Few serious birdwatchers would miss the chance to visit Florida's Everglades but what they may not realise is that most of Florida is superb for birdwatching. In all, 430 species have been noted and studied, with rarities such as caracaras, sandhill cranes, and vagrants from the West Indies.

Birdwatching in Florida is excellent all year round, though summer is usually the quietest time. There is a huge diversity of bird habitats to choose from – prairies, pinelands, scrub, pine-oak woodlands, the vast swamps of Big Cypress and the Everglades, marshes, shoreline, barrier islands, rivers and mangrove swamps.

Overall, spring is the best season, from mid-March to mid-May. The central four weeks are the high point. Before then many of the brilliant summer species may not have arrived from the tropics.

The spring and autumn migrations, when birds in their thousands head north or south, are very exciting. A sudden cold spell can also bring in thousands of passage birds, pausing for better weather. These are land birds for the most part, though in autumn the shores may be thick with waders.

The autumn migration is not usually as fascinating as the spring. It is slower and more gradual with fewer numbers in total, and many birds are devoid of their bright breeding plumage.

Winter is excellent. Waders such as the long-legged herons, ibis, storks and spoonbills (the last easily recognised by its great spatula of a bill) stand motionless, or stalk like automata, their long bills making lightning stabs into the water to rise with a fish.

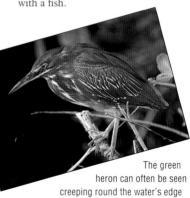

The green heron can often be seen creeping round the water's edge

A sandhill crane

A roseate spoonbill stands motionless

Bald cypresses at Corkscrew Swamp

Snowy egret

Shopping

'Shop till you drop' is a phrase you may tire of hearing in Florida. Americans have elevated shopping into an art form and almost into a religion. For many European visitors, it is a real treat as many things are cheap compared to prices at home.

Just looking

Florida's reputation for the exclusive names in American shopping is high. In the southeast, few would want to miss a stroll down Worth Avenue in Palm Beach, even if it's only to window shop

Mallory Square, a Key West marketplace

along this 'millionaires' row', where the rich and famous buy. That also makes it a good place for 'people watching', and the chances of spotting a film star, a politician, a public figure, or a member of a royal house (no matter how obscure) are good.

The exclusive square mile of Bal Harbour, north of Miami Beach, is another mecca for the serious browser, with names such as Saks Fifth Avenue, Neiman Marcus, Cartier, Schwarz, Nancy Heller, Gucci, Louis Vuitton, Brooks Brothers and Bottega Veneta and Fiori's of Italy. It's a pleasure just to stroll in such a luxurious mall and, when your feet get tired, relax on a wooden seat in walkways lined with tropical plants.

Las Olas Boulevard in Fort Lauderdale is another famous Florida shopping name, full of unusual one-off boutiques, famous for jewellery, *haute couture*, art and antiques.

Malls and markets

Throughout the 1980s, Florida saw a huge increase in the number of shopping centres, arcades, malls and galleries. Bayside Market in downtown Miami is a fine example of the genre. Shady seats under awnings look out to old-fashioned ships and modern excursion boats. Since 1993, there is also Miami's first Hard Rock Cafe. In malls and markets like this, street entertainment, restaurants

and cafés, and colourful hand-carts dispensing juice and coffee, mingle with luxury boutiques and shops, to make shopping a family recreational activity.

Another excellent waterfront complex is Jacksonville Landing. This market extravaganza has around 120 shops and places set in a horseshoe-shaped building with a large open terrace area that overlooks the St John's River. It claims to cater for every taste and every whim and a brief tour shows it covers most things.

Bargains galore

But never mind famous names and high prices. For many, Florida's greatest attraction is low prices with many good-value department store chains such as Montgomery Ward, J C Penney, Sears and Dillards. The best bargains are in

This mall in Orlando is typical of Florida's shopping complexes – attractive, lively and very entertaining

the specialist discount stores. These are particularly good for clothes, glass, furniture, knick-knacks of every kind, and brand names and designer labels at a fraction of the full price. Stocks may be limited in sizes and colours but are heavily reduced.

Fashion bargain hunters, looking for French labels such as Yves St Laurent, Dior and Cardin, should head for northwest Miami's fashion district, where more than 500 clothing factories have made their home. Many manufacturers run their own outlet stores which feature discontinued lines and seconds (usually very good quality).

From ethnic to upmarket

Tampa has a wide range of shopping possibilities. Historical and ethnic interests are catered for at Ybor Square – three large blocks, once a cigar factory, set around a cobbled square. Characterful specialist shops sell everything from Cuban clothes, gourmet food and inexpensive jewellery to hand-rolled cigars.

Antiques may be found in the cluster of shops on Interbay Peninsula (between MacDill and El Prado Avenues) with beautiful English and French furniture and some Tiffany ware.

Jacobsen's department store in the exclusive Hyde Park Village on Bayshore Boulevard is worth a visit, and here you will find international names such as Benetton, Laura Ashley and Godiva Chocolatier.

Themed shopping

Many shopping areas are much more

Buying sponges at Tarpon Springs. For those with a taste for souvenir-hunting, it needn't just be T-shirts

than just a collection of shops. They are themed areas, 'experiences' or 'villages', either in renovated historical settings or in many cases simply created from scratch. Browse in a 'New England Fishing Village' near Clearwater, a 'Greek Sponge Market' at Tarpon Springs, or a 'turn-of-the-century small town American Main Street' in Kissimmee.

One of the best is Orlando's Church Street Station, where an old railroad and hotel have been converted to an excellent shopping and entertainment centre. Of course, every theme park also has its own shops, so you can come home clutching a cuddly killer whale from Sea World, a cute King Kong from Universal Studios, or almost any character Disney ever dreamed of.

WHAT TO BUY

Apart from clothes, there are many products that are good generally in America, and Florida is no exception.

Books

Books of all sorts, and from many countries, are almost always good value. Even newly published books can be heavily discounted. **Crown Books** is a big discount chain.

Cameras, film and photography

You can buy good cheap cameras in Florida, though you may find the model numbers slightly different, even when a camera, video camera, lens, or whatever, is the same. Look at local photography magazines to get an idea of the price you should expect to pay. Film of all sorts is very low in price and, unless you have a very special and unusual favourite, it's worth buying most of your film stock once you're there. Developing is also cheap and very swift.

Wares of every kind and quality can be found in Key West's Duval Street

Ethnic foods and goods

Try Little Haiti's Caribbean Marketplace and Little Havana in Miami, or Ybor City for Cuban wares and cigars. Key West is also good for the latter.

Music

You will find plenty of compact discs and cassette tapes of every sort of music at good prices. Try **Music 4 Less** in Orlando.

Shelling out

Commercial shells are usually picked live. This has put some sea creatures in danger, and you may like to think about this fact, and also be aware that many shells actually come from far outside Florida.

Gifts with a difference

Museum shops are some of the best retail outlets for unusual, tasteful gifts that reflect something of Florida's history and cultural diversity. In many cases you can visit the shop without paying to see the museum.

KEY WEST
Audubon House
Excellent prints of Audubon birds and natural history subjects.
Whitehead and Greene Streets.

Dansk Family Outlet
Beautiful Scandinavian tableware at low prices. (Also in other cities.)
400 Duval Street.

Fast Buck Freddie's
An interesting variety of unusual items.
431 Duval Street.

Haitian Art Co
The largest selection of Haitian paintings, sculptures and papier-maché objects in the US.
600 Frances Street.

Key West Hand Print
Printed fabrics and fashion. Occasional factory tours and fashion shows.
201 Simonton Street.

Tourist paraphernalia and souvenirs on sale in Key West

Kino Sandals
Selling hand-made sandals since 1966.
Kino Plaza, off Duval Street.

Pirates World
Unusual gold jewellery is designed and made here.
1 Front Street.

MIAMI
Bayside To-Go
Bayside T-shirts, mugs, posters and other unique gifts.
Bayside Marketplace, 401 Biscayne Boulevard.

CocoWalk
One of Miami's leading shopping malls, with outdoor cafés, cinemas, clubs too. Shops include Banana Republic and The Gap.
Coconut Grove.

The Falls Shopping Center
More than 60 shops, including a Bloomingdale's, in a tropical setting, with bridges and waterfalls.
8888 Howard Avenue, Kendall. US–1/136th Street.

The Golfe Shoppe
Well-known makes of clubs, shoes, gloves, clothing, gifts, all at discount prices.
4542 SW 7th Avenue (S Miami, 10 minutes from International Airport).

Lincoln Road Mall
The mall's stores line an open-air pedestrianised zone. A popular place for shopping of all kinds.
16th Street and Lincoln Road, Miami Beach.

Mayfair in the Grove
Exclusive atrium-styled promenade with stores like Yves St Laurent and Ralph Lauren, as well as élite restaurants and nightclubs.
2911 Grand Avenue, Coconut Grove.

ORLANDO
Church Street Station
Shop in a Victorian atmosphere with many fascinating speciality stores and themed restaurants.
124 W Pine Street.

Disney Village Market Place
Leisurely shopping alongside Buena Vista Lagoon, with items from around the world and some of the best souvenirs in Disney. Artisans demonstrate their skills.
Disney World Resort, Lake Buena Vista.

Flea Market Outlet, Inc
Rain or shine, every day over 400 dealers sell their goods all under one roof.
4301 W Vine Street, Kissimmee.

Market Place
Outdoor shopping area with post office, bakery, pharmacy and one-hour film processing.
7600 Dr Phillips Boulevard.

Old Town
A turn-of-the-century boulevard of 70 small speciality shops plus restaurants, bars and tourist attractions.
Highway 192, Kissimmee.

TAMPA
Belz Factory Outlet Mall
Around 170 shops with designer goods at budget prices.
Junction I–4 and Buffalo Avenue.

Eastlake Square Mall
Over 115 shops and restaurants including Montgomery Ward, Belk-Lindsey and J C Penney.
56th St E at Hillsborough Avenue.

Harbour Island
Waterfront shopping, dining and entertainment, with speciality stores.
601 S Harbor Island Boulevard.

Old Hyde Park Village
Some 60 speciality and international stores and restaurants. Many exclusive names including Polo/Ralph Lauren, Brooks Brothers etc.
On Swann and Dakota, near Bayshore.

University Square Mall
Over 130 shops including Burdines, Maison Blanche, J C Penney and Sears, plus four cinemas, and restaurants. Good for toys.
E Fowler Avenue/22nd Street.

Entertainment and the Arts

*F*lorida is not just about rock music, discos, clubs, dinner entertainment and themed attractions. You can find culture too. These days there is also theatre, ballet, opera and classical music. All major venues stage performing arts, pop and rock music and variety shows with top quality national and international performers.

CINEMAS

Films are shown everywhere, from drive-in movies where you park and plug the sound into your car to multi-cinema complexes such as CocoWalk in the heart of Miami's Coconut Grove. Local papers give daily lists of the latest films.

Sarasota's Opera House. The town has a reputation as a cultural centre

DINNER ENTERTAINMENT

MIAMI AND THE SOUTHEAST
Improv
CocoWalk's comedy showcase and dinner.
Coconut Grove. Tel: (305) 441–8200.

Jan McArt's Royal Dinner Theatre
Broadway shows and gourmet dining.

Boca Raton. Tel: (407) 392–3755.

Mai-Kai

South Seas dinner show with Samoan Fire Dancers and exotic atmosphere.
Fort Lauderdale. Tel: (305) 947–9052.

Murder Theatre Inc

Murder mystery dinner.
Riviera Beach. Tel: (407) 863–7723.

ORLANDO

Orlando has turned dinner theatre into a new art with some imaginative settings.

Broadway at the Top

Big bands, music show.
Disney's Contemporary Resort, Lake Buena Vista. Tel: (407) 824–4321.

Fort Liberty

Good old-fashioned Western entertainment.
Kissimmee. Tel: (407) 351–5151.

Medieval Times Dinner and Tournament

Watch jousting as you dine on a medieval-style dinner (no utensils).
Kissimmee. Tel: (407) 396–1518.

Pleasure Island

Every night a New Year's Eve street party.
Disney Village. Tel: (407) 824–4321.

Sleuths Mystery Dinner Show

Solve the mystery while you dine.
Downtown Orlando. Tel: (407) 824–4321.

TAMPA

Columbia Restaurant

Superb Spanish/Cuban food with flamenco dancing in Florida's oldest restaurant.
Ybor City. Tel: (813) 248–4961.

Matterhorn Hofbrau Haus

Oktoberfest atmosphere, with international show.
E Skagway. Tel: (813) 932–0780.

GAMBLING

Only the *pari-mutuel* gaming system (where winners share in the total amount wagered less the management commission) is allowed under Florida law and is applied to certain sporting events. All other gambling is forbidden and the only chance you will have to play in the casino is on a cruise ship outside the Florida state jurisdiction.

Cruise lines with casinos:

Crown Cruise Line

Palm Beach. Tel: (800) 841–7447 (Freephone).

Nieuw Amsterdam (Holland America Line)

Tampa. Tel: (206) 281–3535.

Royal Caribbean Cruise Line

Miami. Tel: (305) 379–4731.

Family entertainment at Fort Liberty

LIVE MUSIC CLUBS, DISCOS AND NIGHTCLUBS

There are hundreds of blues, rock and music clubs and discos, also salsa, Latin and other exotics, mostly, but not all, in Miami Beach. Many continue as night clubs up to 5am. There's usually a happy hour and, particularly at weekends, a dining cover charge.

Rosie O'Grady's, a lively Orlando nightspot with a variety of music

MIAMI AND THE SOUTHEAST

Alcazaba

A Miami legend – high-energy disco with a Latin emphasis.
Coral Gables. Tel: (305) 441–1234.

The Breakers

Big band atmosphere and nightly entertainment. Jackets required.
Palm Beach. Tel: (407) 655–6611.

Club Nu

Claims to be one of the world's top 20 nightclubs. International celebrities; scantily-clad dancers. Well-heeled patrons.
245 22nd Street, South Miami Beach. Tel: (305) 672–0068.

Façade Nightclub

Large dance club/disco with a 10-piece showband, a multi-million-dollar light, video and sound show and a sunken dance floor.
North Miami Beach. Tel: (305) 948–6868.

Las Olas del Malecon

Latin to Top 40.
Howard Johnson Resort Hotel, Miami Beach. Tel: (305) 861–5222.

Music Room

1930s New York-style speakeasy. Local jazz.
Art Deco District. Tel: (305) 531–0392.

Penrod's Beach Club

Rock to Top 40. Shows. Live music/beach parties weekends.
1st Street and Ocean Drive, Miami Beach. Tel: (305) 538–1111.

Regine's

Sophisticated nightlife for yuppies.

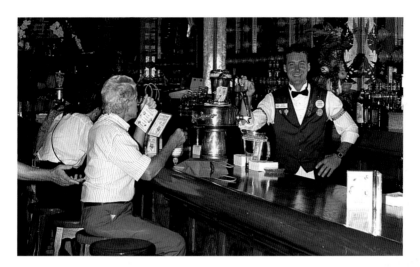

Multi-million-dollar Art Deco splendour. *2669 South Bayshore Drive, Coconut Grove. Tel: (305) 858–9500.*

Studio One 83

Wide range, jazz to disco dancing. Live concerts.
NW 183rd Street, Carol City. Tel: (305) 621–7295.

Tobacco Road

The city's oldest bar, restaurant and night venue and the region's premier blues showcase.
626 S Miami Avenue, Downtown Miami. Tel: (305) 374–1198.

ORLANDO

Church Street Station

This magnificently restored turn-of-the-century railroad station complex stages 20 live shows every night. Two Old West saloons serve up Dixieland and Country and Western, or you can dance to rock 'n' roll classics in a Victorian Crystal

Rosie O'Grady's – part of the Church Street Station complex

Palace, hear folk and bluegrass in Apple Annie's pretty courtyard or go along to Phileas Fogg's high-energy discotheque. *Church Street Station complex. Tel: (407) 422–2434.*

Little Darlin's Rock 'N' Roll Palace

Fifties-style complex with live rock 'n' roll music and a 24-foot-high juke box. *Kissimmee. Tel: (407) 396–6499.*

ST PETERSBURG

Cha Cha Coconuts

A tropical-style bar set on the roof of the Pier. Live rock, jazz and reggae bands. *The Pier, St Petersburg. Tel: (813) 822–6655.*

The Hurricane Lounge

Famous for its live jazz, this three-storey restaurant also puts on discos. *St Petersburg Beach. Tel: (813) 260–4875.*

PERFORMING ARTS

ST PETERSBURG AREA

The **Ruth Eckerd Hall** at Clearwater puts on a wide programme of Broadway shows, theatre, ballet and popular and classical music. The **American Stage Company**, tel: (813) 822–8814, is St Petersburg's professional theatre company and performs from October to June. The **Boatyard Village Theatre**, tel: (813) 536–8299, at the Old Boatyard Village adjacent to the airport, produces modern classics and contemporary dramas.

MIAMI AND THE SOUTHEAST

On the southeast coast, the arts have blossomed. Today, **Burt Reynolds' Jupiter Theatre** incorporates the Burt Reynolds Institute for Theatre Training, tel: (407) 833–7888, and features guest stars along with young aspiring actors in drama, musicals and comedy. Pavarotti has sung with the **Palm Beach Opera**, which produces three grand operas a year. **Ballet Florida**, tel: (407) 844–2900, and **Miami City Ballet**, tel: (813) 532–4880, a young classical company which is one of America's 10 largest, also perform locally.

The 50-year-old **Greater Miami Opera**, tel: (813) 854–7890, sings opera in its original language. The **Florida Philharmonic Orchestra**, tel: (305) 568–2110, attracts many international soloists and plays classical, pop and children's programmes all over the southeast. Miami Beach's **New World Symphony**, tel: (305) 673–3331, is an advanced training orchestra for young professional musicians based at the

Florida offers theatre, opera and ballet as well as the more familiar fare of discos and rock music

restored Art Deco Lincoln Theatre in Miami Beach. Here, you can be among the first to recognise young talent before it becomes famous.

Broadway productions

All over the southeast, you will find pre-Broadway productions, and in many parts of Florida there are seasons of Broadway in the Sunshine. Contact **Ticketmaster**, tel: (813) 358–5885, for Greater Miami tickets (sports events too). Read the Friday edition of *Miami Herald* to find out what's on, or call (407) 471–2901 which also gives information for Greater Palm Beach.

ORLANDO

Orlando's ballet and opera companies and the Florida Symphony Orchestra all use the **Bob Carr Performing Arts Center**, tel: (407) 849–2577. This is also a venue for Broadway series and other shows.

Within Greater Orlando, **Rollins College**, in Winter Park, is home to music and theatre, and has regular recitals and concerts (often free) in the Cornell Fine Arts Museum galleries, tel: (407) 646–2233. Its **Annie Russell Theatre**, tel: (407) 646–2145, has an ambitious summer repertory season and a winter programme. A lovely setting for music is the **Knowles Chapel**, tel: (407) 646–2115, with an annual Bach festival.

For information read the Calendar section of Friday's *Orlando Sentinel*. Also pick up the free magazine, *See Orlando*.

TAMPA

The **Tampa Bay Performing Arts Center**, box office tel: (813) 221–1045, stages world-class performances of music, dance and theatre and is home to

Live entertainment is a big draw

several Tampa-based groups, including the **Florida Orchestra**, tel: (813) 221–4774, the **Tampa Oratorio Society**, tel: (813) 988–2165, and the Tampa Players, tel: (813) 229–1505. The **Tampa Theatre** movie palace, tel: (813) 223–8981, still shows films, and stages concerts, and other events. The **Ritz Theatre**, Ybor City, tel: (813) 247–PLAY, presents both mainstream and fringe.

For information the *Tampa Tribune*'s Friday edition has lists of arts, entertainment and nightlife. Ticketmaster's ticket number is (813) 287–8844. Arts Line information is on (813) 229–ARTS.

Children

*F*lorida is without a doubt America's number-one children's state. Almost everything to see and do here is designed for families. For growing youngsters, there's the challenge of thrill rides, and everyone loves the water parks with their daring, twisting tunnels. Getting around the parks with toddlers is easy. Pushchairs are usually available free of charge and many parks run little trains and trams to save your feet. Many evening entertainments are fun for the whole family and children can be included in most cases.

LEARNING IS FUN, FUN IS LEARNING

'Hands-on' applied to a museum is a description you often see in a brochure or booklet about Florida. It means that children – and unselfconscious adults too – can try out their skill on a range of weird apparatus and exhibits.

The underlying purpose is always educational but the feeling is fun. So in St Petersburg's Great Explorations, for example, the way in which light can be 'bent' into producing an optical illusion is demonstrated when you enter a box and see your head served up on a platter in the mirror! Many exhibits are literally hands-on, however, solving simple tests of logic, pushing buttons on a computer keyboard and so on. It may sound dry but adults are usually just as hooked as children on the ingenious 'stations' that the new generation of interactive museums/'Discovery Centers' are now introducing.

FAMILY FOOD

Except for the ritziest establishments, nearly all restaurants and cafés make a point of appealing to families with

Feeding time for a dolphin at Sea World in Orlando

children's menus and portions. An

Dwarf Village at Busch Gardens, Tampa

impressive sight in many of the theme parks is the absence of litter and the way people take it for granted that they return trays and cutlery and put the scraps in the designated area, a lesson for many overseas visitors.

Orlando can claim the title of being the 'Capital of Kids' Florida'. Quite apart from Disney World, there are so many choices of theme parks and family outings that it is almost impossible to decide. It's not cheap, however. All the major theme parks assume that you will spend the whole day with them and have a relatively high entrance fee but, after that, all the rides are free and you only pay for your food and drink. So, always take into account what a price includes. You can easily spend a full day at each of the Disney parks, Sea World, Universal Studios, Busch Gardens, Silver Springs and Cypress Gardens.

To see animals and brightly coloured birds at close quarters fascinates most children and, for those who are already interested in wildlife, a canoe or airboat ride in one of the swampy areas reveals something new at every turn. The numerous springs are also good for close-ups of wildlife, and this can be such a thrill that you may see excited youngsters tugging complete strangers over to the water's edge to point out the great blurred shape of a manatee.

Even modest hotels and campsites will have pools where youngsters gather. The bucket-and-spade brigade will love the quieter coast and island beaches of the west, but teenagers may prefer the buzz and flurry of some of the east coast beaches, with action-packed fairgrounds and amusement arcades and lots of stalls selling beach shirts, and soft drinks.

Florida should make for a perfect family holiday. Remember, however, that it does get very hot, particularly in summer when humidity is also uncomfortably high. Make sure you drink plenty of water, and never forget the sun screen cream.

Florida – The State for Sports

*F*lorida claims to have some 1,000 golf courses and that must be enough for even the most dedicated golf fanatic. Palm Beach County alone has 130 golf courses and is home to the Professional Golfers' Association. The other main sport is tennis, with countless courts everywhere. It goes without saying that pool, lake or sea swimming is everywhere but many hotel-resorts are based on golf and tennis and a smaller number have equestrian centres.

One of three courses at Grenelefe Resort

GOLF AND TENNIS RESORTS

Grenelefe Resort, a 30-minute drive from Orlando, has three first-class golf courses and world-class tennis. For around 10 years the resort's Robert Trent Jones West Course, 7,325 yards in length, has featured as either Florida's number one or two in the golfing magazine *Golf Digest*. Many guests play 36 holes a day, but there are other activities: five natural free-form swimming pools, fishing, and boating, all based on Lake Marian.
Tel: (407) 471–3995.

Indian River Plantation, an up-market resort on Hutchinson Island on the Treasure Coast, has an 18-hole par-61 golf course and a dozen or so superb tennis courts. Its marina rents power-

boats for deep-sea fishing, and there are cycling and jogging trails.
Tel: (407) 225–3700.

Key West has an 18-hole, par-72 golf course on Stock Island, but the Keys are prime islands for sub-aqua diving, with amazing marine life on the offshore reefs in places such as the John Pennekamp Coral Reef State Park and the National Marine Sanctuary off Key Largo.

Palm Beach Golf-a-Round is a chance to sample the area's 10 best golf courses, with one round daily at each of the resorts taking part.
Details from Palm Beach Visitors' Bureau, tel: (407) 471–3995.

Walt Disney World has five 18-hole championship golf courses and 15 tennis courts. There is also speed-boat driving on a 'mini' scale, sailing and horse riding on offer. *Tel: (407) 824–2270.*

Tennis is a major sport in the States

World of Golf Tours is one of the biggest packagers of international golf tours, and worth contacting.
231 Semoran Commerce Plaza, Suite 105, Apoka, FL, 32703-4670. Tel: (407) 884–8300.

Golf information from: Florida State Golf Association, PO Box 211777, Sarasota, FL 34276.
Tel: (813) 921–5695.

The golf resort at Port St Lucie

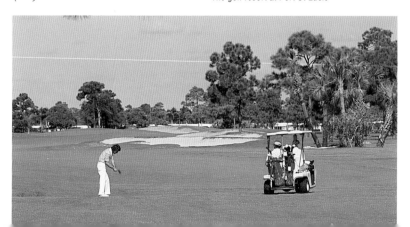

SAILING AND BOATING

Almost every village, resort or town by the sea has a marina and a public boat harbour. You can hire boats in a wide range of sizes, from dinghies to ocean cruisers in the larger resorts. Wind-surfing and water-skiing are popular all around the coasts and on many of the bigger lakes. Resorts and towns will have surfboards, waterskis and all the necessary equipment for hire and there are many companies, as well as dive shops which specialise in sub-aqua equipment and often provide tours, boats and guides. Hotels usually have information on local fishing trips.

Florida's Canoe Trail System has 36 routes, all marked, along main rivers, creeks and streams, often in state and national parks. Some companies also arrange canoe tours. Enquire at area tourist offices. A useful leaflet is *Florida Recreational Canoe Trails* from the Department of Natural Resources, Division of Recreation and Parks, 3900

Masterly control of a Hobie Cat

Commonwealth Boulevard, Tallahassee, FL 32399–3000.

SUB-AQUA

The southeast coast and the Keys are the prime places for snorkelling and scuba diving, with amazing marine life on the offshore reefs in dozens of places.

Biscayne National Park, John Pennekamp Coral Reef State Park and the National Marine Sanctuary off Key Largo are three favourites. Since 1987, the Keys have been forming artificial reefs. First two old Coast Guard cutters were sunk; then in 1993 a complete Boeing 727 began to acquire marine life in 79 feet of water off Key Biscayne.

Dive shops hire out equipment and provide information about tours, boats and general safety procedures. Scuba calls for a Certified Divers' Card and, without one, you will have to take a day (or shorter) course.

SPORTS IN NATIONAL AND STATE PARKS

The big state and national parks are quite different from urban parks. They may cover thousands of acres and their objective is to retain the land or water in the condition it was when Europeans first arrived in Florida. In many, canoeing, boating, fishing, snorkelling and scuba diving are welcome and some have good horse-riding routes and walking trails. It is often possible to hire canoes.

Canoeing in the wilderness

Among the most spectacular canoe trails is the 100-mile-long Wilderness Waterway. It starts at Flamingo on Florida Bay and twists its way north through wide-spreading estuaries and sea, past Sandfly Island to the ranger station at Chokoloskee Bay, close to Everglades City. You can camp overnight, but don't forget that this requires a back-country camping permit, from ranger stations. There are half a dozen shorter trails, up to 12 miles in length, and river canoeing around Everglades City.

Riding trails

At least a dozen state parks have good riding trails, many with horses to hire and stable accommodation. In some areas the Floridians have also converted disused railroad tracks into trails, and one of the best for horses is the **Tallahassee-St Marks Historic Railroad Trail** (tel: (904) 925–6216). Once it transported cotton and other goods from north Florida to south Georgia, but now the 16 miles that follow the historic route to St Marks make good riding.

You may see joggers and cyclists on

Getting away from it all in a canoe

the way, but nothing with an engine. **Sea Horse Stables** on Anastasia Island north of Jacksonville is one of the few places with horse riding on the beach. Tel: (904) 261–4878.

The *Florida State Parks Guide* is published by the Department of Natural Resources (see address on page 160). General sports information is available from Florida's Sports Development Office, Room 455, Collins Building, Tallahassee, Florida 32399–2000. Tel: (904) 488–8347.

A PASSION FOR FISHING

Many people will tell you that they moved to Florida just for the fishing; others come every year to take part in the sport, be it in fresh or saltwater.

Some 6.5 million acres, or 17 per cent of the state is covered by lake, marsh and estuary. In fact there are so many rivers, streams, canals and lakes that no one is further than 10 miles from somewhere to wet a fishing line. On the long coastline all around this peninsular state, anglers by the thousand patiently extend their lines from piers that jut out over the sea every few miles.

Florida has no closed season for freshwater fish and the daily 'bag' limit is generous, with some 115 native species including bream, bass and perch to tempt the most restless angler. Nearly a million anglers apply for freshwater licences each year.

From early morning, fly and light tackle enthusiasts push across Florida Bay for snook, sea trout and tarpon in the flats and channels around Flamingo. Others set out for blackfin tuna, dolphin (the fish, not the mammal of the same name) or, the greatest thrill of all, a blue marlin, which can average up to 200 pounds and is more often seen or even hooked, than caught.

In all, with 175 marine and exotic species to add to the 115 freshwater, whether you fish inland, from shore or at sea, it's hard to have other than a successful day.

Getting the bug at an early age

The calm of an inland waterway

Setting off to sea from Boca Raton

Deep-sea fishing at sunset

SPECTATOR SPORTS

AMERICAN FOOTBALL
College football is immensely popular in Florida, and thousands turn out for an important game. There are also three professional teams. **Miami Dolphins**, Joe Robbie Stadium (September to December), tel: (305) 620–2578. **Tampa Bay Buccaneers**, Tampa, tel: (813) 879–BUCS. **Orlando Thunder**, tel: (407) 422–1616.

BASEBALL
Professional baseball is largely confined to pre-season spring training of the northern teams, but Florida's first professional team, the Miami Marlins, has now taken to the field. Other native teams may follow as cities vie to encourage them.

BASKETBALL
There are two professional teams – **Miami Heat**, Miami Arena, NW 1st Avenue, tel: (305) 577–4328, and **Orlando Magic**, Orlando Arena, tel: (407) 896–2442 – plus many more amateur teams.

JAI ALAI
An interesting 1935 introduction from the Basque country is the ancient game of jaialai. Pronounced 'high-a-lie', this is the world's fastest-moving ball game, played by two or four players on a squash-style court called a *fronton*. A basket-like glove is strapped to the wrist and the players catch and hurl a ball at speeds of up to 188mph. It is highly popular, with *frontons* in most bigger cities.

EQUESTRIAN SPORTS
Although Florida is not renowned for horse racing, it does boast one of the world's most beautiful racecourses, at Hialeah Park, Miami. The thoroughbred racing season runs from mid-November to late May.

Calder Race Course, NW 27th Avenue, Miami, is another attractive meet.

The Pompano Harness Track, on Race Track Road, Pompano Beach, tel: (305) 972–2000, offers the only

Baseball – one of the US's premier sports and a national pastime

opportunity in Florida for the elegant and exciting sport of harness racing, from October to mid-April.

Horse racing began early, and legend has it that Hernando de Soto's party raced their horses in Cuba before leaving for Florida. With them they brought many fine beasts of royal Spanish stock. By the 1840s the state had three courses, the Marion Course near Tallahassee, the Franklin Course at Apalachicola and one near present-day St Joe's.

THE CAPITAL OF SPEED

Daytona Beach is synonymous world-wide with car racing, from the early pioneer days along the beach to the magnificent stadium opened in 1959. In 1903, Alexander Winton broke the record with his 'Bullet' car, at an astonishing 68mph. Daytona's most prestigious races include the Daytona 500, the 24-hour SunBank 24 for sports cars and, for motorbikes, the Daytona 200.

In February, the streets of downtown

Autoracing at Sebring, home of the Grand Prix Sports Car 12-hour Endurance Test

Miami become a Grand Prix race track with drivers from many countries.

GREYHOUND RACING

The St Petersburg Kennel Club, which started in 1924, is the oldest greyhound track still in use in North America, and the sport's popularity has continued with greyhound racing in every area of the state. In the northwest you will find tracks at Pensacola, Monticello and Ebro, while Jacksonville is the northeast's main centre.

In the west there are tracks at St Petersburg, Sarasota and Tampa, and further south at Bonita Springs. In the southeast, it is no surprise to find greyhound racing in Palm Beach, Fort Lauderdale and Miami, and Key West also has a track.

Sports details from: Florida Division of Tourism, 566 Collins Building, Tallahassee, Florida 32399–2000.

Food and Drink

Eating out

Ask a chef in any good restaurant or hotel whether there is a special Florida cuisine, and the answer is likely to be whatever is the style of that particular restaurant. In fact, the only real Florida dish that you are likely to come across is the ubiquitous Key lime pie. The Florida menu is as diverse and derivative as the many cultures that make up the state itself.

From the halcyon days of the big cattle industry, Floridians have been meat eaters, so if in doubt, a steak, usually served in very generous portions is nearly always a good choice. So too are burgers. The restaurant variety is often infinitely better than its 'thin' fast-

Good restaurants in Florida are legion

food relative. Just to make purists shudder, it has to be admitted that 'veggieburgers' are now almost as common on menus as the traditional full-blooded form. Mexican food, hot and tasty, is very popular, particularly in the south, from *quesadillas* to *enchiladas* and fierce sauces such as the green-tinted *muy*, best washed down with cold water. It is a mixture of early Indian foods and Spanish cooking, although the latter is now almost totally dominant. Favourites include paella and *arroz con pollo* (chicken cooked in wine and spices, served with yellow rice). Plantains and black beans are common accompaniments. Try it in Little Havana in Miami, or in Ybor City in Tampa. But you can get ethnic food anywhere in Florida. Chinese, Italian, Cajun/Creole (Louisiana-style cooking) and Japanese are all highly visible on the main highways and in the food courts.

Eating in the parks

Though the theme parks sometimes seem to be filled with thousands of strolling crowds, stuffing themselves with ice cream, popcorn, cookies, crisps (potato chips) and the rest, almost all have restaurants at different price levels, (generally pricier than those outside the parks). Nevertheless, it has to be said that everything in the garden is not always tasty. Although restaurants will be clean, tidy and well staffed, food quality ranges from average to often poor and over-priced. The superb restaurants of EPCOT's World Showcase are a shining exception to the general theme-park rule, and although these are not cheap they are usually excellent value.

From the sea and lake

As Florida is surrounded on three sides by saltwater and boasts thousands of lakes and good fishing rivers, it is no surprise that fish and seafood are a pleasure wherever you go. Try yellowtail, pompano, grouper, scrod and dolphin. Don't worry, the last one is rather an ugly fish, completely separate from the performing mammals you enjoyed at Sea World!

The Florida conch (pronounced conk), with its lacy pink shells around chewy sea meat, has even given its name to Keys people, particularly the inhabitants of Key West. The stone crab season lasts from mid-October to mid-May and stocks are self-renewing. By tradition, fishermen break off one claw only and throw the crab back into the water where it regrows the missing claw (those in the know assure you that it doesn't hurt!). The quintessential plate

Florida beaches offer plenty of opportunities for organised family picnicking and barbecuing

of stone crab claw comes hot or cold but always with a sharp mustard sauce.

Oysters are abundant and not too expensive, usually harvested from the 10,000-acre oyster beds of Apalachicola Bay. Purists eat them raw in their shells, often at 'raw bars' which also serve a whole variety of cooked and uncooked seafood. Florida scallops, plentiful on the Gulf Coast from Pensacola to the Pinellas, are smaller and sweeter than the deep-sea variety, but still good.

Variations on the classic fish soup *bouillabaisse* are popular, and there are dozens of types of fish, steamed, grilled or cooked in the oven. Wherever you go, you can eat beside or even on the water, with pier and verandah restaurants, and dining cruises.

Most cafés serve excellent breakfasts

Breakfast and brunch

There is nothing to beat an American breakfast, and the price is almost always a delight to Europeans. One example illustrates thousands of others: the Front Porch Café on Ocean Drive in Miami Beach, where you can sit and watch the sea, serves a Beach Breakfast Bonanza of three scrambled eggs cooked with cheese, tomatoes, mushrooms, onions and peppers, served with fresh fruit and raisin pumpernickel toast, for just a few dollars. Virginia Honey Baked Ham is just an extra 50 cents. Another bonus in

almost all Florida establishments is the 'bottomless cup of coffee'. Once you've paid for a coffee, the waiter will return again and again at no extra charge.

Sunday brunch is just as much of a Florida tradition as it is throughout the US. It is a huge meal, taking in the ingredients of a big breakfast and a good lunch, often with a musical entertainment from traditional jazz to Latin American, and a cocktail-of-the-day. Hotels, restaurants and cruise boats all specialise in brunch. American plates are almost always heaped high, and it is quite acceptable to ask for a 'doggy bag'. It is also quite normal for two people to share a starter or a dessert. Most places let you take as much as you like from the salad bar, and this is usually eaten prior to the *entrée* as a course in its own right.

WHERE TO EAT

The following list is a brief selection of places in the most popular areas. The prices below are for a main dinner, including coffee, but without drinks or tips:

Cheap and cheerful (**CC**) – $8 or below
Moderate (**M**) – $8-$15
Expensive (**E**) – $16-$25
Very expensive (**VE**) – $25 upwards

ORLANDO
(VE) Dux

A mixture of American and international. Rated among Central Florida's Top Ten.
Also **Capriccio,** Italian trattoria (**E**).
Both at Peabody Hotel, 9801 International Drive. Tel: (407) 352–4000. Jacket required.

(M) The Grand Floridian Café

Family eating with a tropical flavour. Seafood, chicken, burgers etc.

In the Grand Floridian, Lake Buena Vista.
Tel: (407) 824–8000.

(CC) Numero Uno
The best Cuban in town, famed for
authentic fare.
2499 S Orange Avenue. Tel: (407)
841–3840.

(CC) Paco's
Crowds indicate the success of this
genuine Mexican food, with especially
good tacos in unpretentious
surroundings.
1801 W Fairbanks Avenue, Winter Park.
Tel: (407) 629–0149.

TAMPA
(VE) Bern's Steak House
A classy steak house with an exclusive
wine list.
1208 S Howard Avenue. Tel: (813)
251–2421.

(M) Café Creole and Oyster Bar
Well-spiced Cajun and Creole food in an
historic 19th-century Ybor City
building. Good jazz.
1300 E 9th Avenue. Tel: (813) 247–6283.

(M) The Columbia
A Tampa institution; a selection of
beautiful dining rooms, excellent Cuban
food, and famous flamenco dancing.
2117 7th Avenue, Ybor City. Tel: (813)
248–4961.

(M) Crawdaddy's
A Roaring Twenties atmosphere on the
waterfront. Best for seafood and steaks.
2500 Rocky Point Road. Tel: (813)
281–0407.

Eating al fresco in Florida is a popular
pastime – thanks, in no small measure, to
the year-round sunshine. This is Coconut
Grove in Miami

ST PETERSBURG AND THE PINELLAS

(M) Basta's Ristorante
High-quality North Italian cuisine. Superb pasta, breads and soups.
1625 Fourth Street S, St Petersburg. Tel: (813) 894–7880.

(E-VE) The Bubble Room
Enjoy zany nostalgia and never mind the waistline. Feast on seafood, gigantic steaks, 'bubble bread' and over-the-top desserts.
1500 Captiva Road, Captiva Island. Tel: (813) 472–5588. (No reservations.)

(CC) Doe Al's
Good ol' Southern cooking at its best. Try the country-style pork, fried chicken, catfish, and vegetables such as collard greens, black-eyed peas and sweet potatoes.
85 Corey Circle, St Petersburg Beach. Tel: (813) 360–7976.

(VE) King Charles Room
Ornate waterfront restaurant with luxury French and Continental cuisine. Crystal chandeliers and harpist. Excellent Sunday brunch.
Don CeSar Hotel, 3400 Gulf Road, St Petersburg Beach. Tel: (813) 360–1881. Jacket required.

(M) Mucky Duck
Once an old Florida beach house, now a favourite restaurant with a Swiss owner-chef. Fresh local seafood is the speciality.
2500 Estero Boulevard, Fort Myers Beach. Tel: (813) 463–5519.

(E) Windows on the Water
Gourmet 'Gulfshore cuisine', a blend of Cajun, Creole, Tex Mex and Southern, even alligator sausage, in a seaview restaurant.
Sundial Beach and Tennis Resort, 1451 Middle Gulf Drive, Sanibel Island. Tel: (813) 472–4151.

NORTHEAST COAST

(M-E) Chizu
An authentic taste of Japan, near the ocean.
1227 S 3rd Street, Jacksonville Beach. Tel: (904) 241–8455.

(CC) Conch House
Florida's oldest family owns this sea-deck venue (with its 8,500-palm-frond thatch).
57 Comares Avenue, St Augustine. Tel: (904) 829–8646.

(M) Juliette's Restaurant and Bistro
French regional food and seafood.
Omni Hotel, 245 Water Street, Jacksonville. Tel: (904) 358–7737.

(M) The Monk's Vineyard
Casual dining in an historic area. Try home-made soup, Continental cuisine and vegetarian specialities.
56 St George Street, St Augustine. Tel: (904) 824–5888.

(E) The Wine Cellar
Continental and California *nouvelle cuisine.*
1314 Prudential Drive, Jacksonville. Tel: (904) 398–8989.

MIAMI AND THE SOUTHEAST

(E) A Mano
New American gourmet food in Art Deco setting. Dine outdoors.
Betsy Ross Hotel, 1440 Ocean Drive. Tel: (305) 531–3934.

(CC) Café Tu Tu Tango
Looks like an artist's studio for multi-ethnic food. From crisp fried calamari to spiced chicken wings.
In CocoWalk, 3015 Grand Avenue, Coconut Grove. Tel: (305) 448–6942.

(E-VE) The Dining Galleries
Four dining areas in a beautiful antique setting with *objets d'art* give a European flavour to décor and excellent food. Try Florida pompano and Château-briand.
Fountainebleau Hilton Hotel, 4441 Collins Avenue, Miami Beach. Tel: (305) 538–2000.

(CC) La Carreta
Family-style atmosphere and authentic Cuban food.
3632 SW 8th Street, Little Havana. Tel: (305) 446–4915.

Broiled grapefruit is a traditional dish that can be found on the menu at both lunch and dinner at most eateries

(CC) Woolfie's Gourmet Deli-Restaurant
A Miami Beach kosher classic, with huge menu. Famed meeting place in Art Deco district since 1947.
2038 Collins Avenue. Tel: (305) 538–6626.

(E-VE) Pier House Restaurant
Try scampi in Amaretto and other specialities at one of South Florida's best gourmet restaurants, with a waterfront view.
Its sister restaurant, the **Harbour View Café (M),** serves excellent conch fritters, soups, chowders and fresh seafood.
Pier House Hotel, 1 Duval Street, Key West. Tel: (305) 296–4600.

Hotels and Accommodation

*T*he good news for the average family traveller is that Florida hotels normally charge a price for the room and not per person. This can be tremendous value because it means two adults, plus two children can use one room.

Family comfort

For real economy, choose a family-owned motel, often on the edge of town or on the highway to the beach. These are variable in quality though the basic accommodation will be a comfortable double room, usually with extra beds or sofa beds for up to two children, its own bathroom, phone and, almost inevitably, a television.

A little costlier are the budget-price and moderate-price hotels, almost always part of large all-American or worldwide chains. Two large double beds, air conditioning and a swimming pool are the norm.

The Fontainebleau Hilton at Miami is typical of the area's ultra-modern range of hotels offering every facility and luxury

Resorts and condos

In America a 'resort' does not just imply a place where people go on holiday; it is usually a luxurious holiday hotel, very often with an emphasis on sports and water activities.

A condominium (or a 'condo') is a phrase that also puzzles Europeans. It is an apartment, with a lounge, two or three bedrooms and bathrooms and its own kitchen and balcony, which again is usually part of a large holiday resort.

Ultra de luxe

At the very top end of the hotel range the sky is the limit. Companies vie with each other to produce innovations and new luxuries to lure well-heeled guests. But despite that, the room rate can still compare favourably with the equivalent European-capital hotel.

Looking after yourselves

Self-catering accommodation comes in all shapes and sizes. There are many well-equipped camping sites serving tents, caravans and campervans (called recreation vehicles, RVs, which you can hire). Camp facilities are good, with all but the cheapest centring on a pool, some form of restaurant and some sport amenities.

Walt Disney World has its own resorts, mostly comprising de-luxe hotels, though in the last few years the company has provided a couple of more modestly priced hotels, and there is camping at Disney's Fort Wilderness campground.

Bed and breakfast inns

An American bed-and-breakfast inn is not a licenced establishment offering accommodation in the European sense; it is a private house along British B & B lines. These are often houses of character, run by couples who have decided to escape the 'rat race' further north, and facilities are usually good within an easy, family atmosphere. Comparatively few areas run this type of establishment, and they can be difficult to arrange until you are there, but always ask. The old city of St Augustine has made a speciality of the bed and breakfast inn; here you could find yourself staying in a charming old house dating back to the 19th century or beyond. The idea is catching on but it is, as yet, not comprehensive. Bed and breakfast prices are also rising.

Rates for accommodation vary enormously between high (winter) and low (summer) season.

Staying at Walt Disney World can be pricey

MIAMI

There is a multitude of world-class hotels, tourist-priced hotels and holiday apartments in the Miami area. You will find it considerably cheaper if you do not require an ocean view. For some of the chains it is possible to pre-purchase accommodation coupons. For central reservation service tel: (800) 950–0232 toll free.

THE KEYS

There are lodges, B&Bs and hotels throughout the Keys, most plentiful in Islamorada and Key West. Many Key West B&Bs are charming old houses; camping areas are prolific in the Lower Keys.

LEE ISLAND COAST

There are many reasonably priced hotels and motels in the area. The best place for family attractions is North Fort Myers.

ORLANDO

You are spoilt for choice here. The number of hotels, motels, resorts and self-catering units available increases each year.

THE PINELLAS

There are hundreds of motels with thousands of rooms in the Pinellas as well as hotels and holiday flats.

TAMPA

Large hotels and self-catering holiday flats are plentiful. All the big chain names are here, including a Hyatt Regency, Marriott, Holiday Inn and Hilton. A boat or helicopter will transport visitors to Bahia Beach Island Resort and Marina in Tampa Bay, a full-service resort with hotel rooms and apartments and a range of sports facilities.

The Polynesian Resort at Walt Disney World

EUROPEAN OFFICES OF MAJOR INTERNATIONAL HOTEL CHAINS
(Based in Britain)

Best Western Hotels
143 London Road, Kingston-upon-Thames, Surrey KT2 6NA.
Tel: (0181) 541–0033.

Days Inn Hotels
59–65 Upper Ground, London SE1 9PQ. Tel: (0171) 633–9392.

Forte Hotels
Forte House, Gateway Road, Aylesbury, Bucks HP19 3EB. Tel: 01345–500400.

Hilton and Conrad Hotels
Suite 104-6, The Chambers, Chelsea Harbour, London SW10 0XF.
Tel: 01800–289303.

Holiday Inn
10-12 New College Parade, Finchley Road, London NW3 5EP.
Tel: (0171) 722–7755.

Howard Johnson Hotels
20 Barclay Road, Croydon, Surrey CR0 1JN. Tel: (0181) 666–1418.

Hyatt Hotels and Resorts
113 Upper Richmond Road, London SW15 2UD. Tel: (0181) 780–1000.

Inter Continental and Forum Hotels
Thameside Centre, Kew Bridge Road, Brentford, Middlesex TW8 0EB.
Tel: (0181) 847–2277.

Marriott Hotels
80 Regent Street, London W1R 6AQ.
Tel: (0171) 439–0281.

The Hilton Hotel in Orlando

Ramada International Hotels
160 Brompton Road, London SW31HS.
Tel: (0171) 235–5264.

Sheraton Hotels, Inns, Resorts,
210 New King's Road, London SW6 4NZ. Tel: 01800–353535.

Westin Hotels and Resorts
7-8 Conduit Street, London W1R 9TG.
Tel: 01800–282565.

The Park Plaza Hotel, Winter Park

Practical Guide

ARRIVING

UK visitors no longer need a visa for less than 90 days in the US (providing you have a return ticket or one for further travel beyond the US), just a full British passport. A visa waiver form I–94W will be given to you to fill in on the aircraft. Hand it with your passport to immigration control. Other nationalities should enquire at the nearest US Embassy well before their journey whether or not they need a visitor's visa. The problems of arriving without one, where it is required, are enormous.

International airports

You will land at Orlando, Tampa or Miami.

Orlando International Airport
1 Airport Boulevard, Orlando, FL 32827–4399. Tel: (407) 826–2001. Seven miles south of Orlando.

Tampa International Airport
PO Box 22287, Tampa, FL 33622. Tel: (813) 276–3400. Five miles west of Tampa.

Miami International Airport
PO Box 592075, AMF-Miami, FL 33159. Tel: (305) 871–7090. Five miles west of downtown Miami.

Northwest Airlines is a major carrier from the UK with daily year-round departures from Gatwick and Glasgow, connecting to 10 Florida cities.

Florida also has international airports at Jacksonville, St Petersburg-Clearwater, Palm Beach and Key West, used by scheduled and charter flights.

Trains and buses

Only from a Northern state would you arrive by Amtrak train, which goes west to Tampa and east to Miami, with two trains per day. They are comfortable with restaurant and sleeping cars.

Amtrak, 60 Massachusetts Avenue, NE, Washington DC 20002. Tel: (202) 906–3000; fax (202) 906–2211. Amtrak hotline tel: 1-8000-USA-RAIL.

If you plan more than one rail

journey, buy a Florida Regional Railpass before you go. Clearwater, St Petersburg and Sarasota are linked by bus.

An Interstate bus, quick and efficient

CAMPING

There are around 700 campsites in Florida, from simple 'back-country' camp sites where an area is marked off for tents and sleeping bags, to sites offering hook-ups (mains connection) for RVs and trailers (campervans and caravans), plus restaurants, sports and recreational facilities. It is possible to hire RVs, though you may have to search for an outlet, and it is usually cheaper to book before you go. Travel agents with good contacts in Florida will be able to arrange this. Seventeen of the 43 state parks which offer camping facilities do not pre-book their sites but operate on a first-come, first-served basis.

Many sites are privately owned, of varying sizes and often family run, in places close to attractions where the demand is: around Orlando-Disney, Daytona, Miami and the southeast.

Camping guides

Florida Campground Association's *Florida Campground Directory* (free of charge) gives details and routes for 200 campsites. Available from the head office at 1638 N Plaza Drive, Tallahassee, FL 32308–5364. Tel: (904) 656–8878. Also ask in tourist information offices. For national and state park camping details, write to the Department of Natural Resources, Division of Recreation and Parks, 3900 Commonwealth Boulevard, Tallahassee, FL 32399–3000.

CLIMATE

Although summer temperatures are much the same throughout Florida (usually in the 80s°F), winter climates can vary. January temperatures range from around 52°F in the northwest to 67°F along the lower coast and 70°F in the Keys.

Weather Chart Conversion
25.4mm = 1 inch
°F = 1.8 × °C + 32

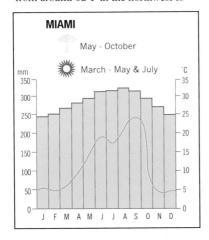

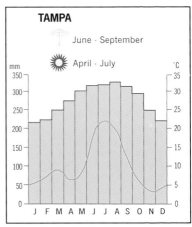

CONVERSION TABLE

FROM	TO	MULTIPLY BY
Inches	Centimetres	2.54
Centimetres	Inches	0.3937
Feet	Metres	0.3048
Metres	Feet	3.2810
Yards	Metres	0.9144
Metres	Yards	1.0940
Miles	Kilometres	1.6090
Kilometres	Miles	0.6214
Acres	Hectares	0.4047
Hectares	Acres	2.4710
Gallons	Litres	4.5460
Litres	Gallons	0.2200
Ounces	Grams	28.35
Grams	Ounces	0.0353
Pounds	Grams	453.6
Grams	Pounds	0.0022

FROM	TO	MULTIPLY BY
Pounds	Kilograms	0.4536
Kilograms	Pounds	2.205
Tons	Tonnes	1.0160
Tonnes	Tons	0.9842

Men's Suits

UK	36	38	40	42	44	46	48
Rest of Europe	46	48	50	52	54	56	58
US	36	38	40	42	44	46	48

Dress Sizes

UK	8	10	12	14	16	18
France	36	38	40	42	44	46
Italy	38	40	42	44	46	48
Rest of Europe	34	36	38	40	42	44
US	6	8	10	12	14	16

Men's Shirts

UK	14	14.5	15	15.5	16	16.5	17
Rest of Europe	36	37	38	39/40	41	42	43
US	14	14.5	15	15.5	16	16.5	17

Men's Shoes

UK		7	7.5	8.5	9.5	10.5	11
Rest of Europe		41	42	43	44	45	46
US		8	8.5	9.5	10.5	11.5	12

Women's Shoes

UK	4.5	5	5.5	6	6.5	7
Rest of Europe	38	38	39	39	40	41
US	6	6.5	7	7.5	8	8.5

CRIME

You'll meet crime in any international city and it is no surprise that Miami has issued one of the best safety leaflets, which recommends that you should follow all your normal safety tips.

Personal safety
ALWAYS be alert.

NEVER leave luggage, bags or briefcases unattended in a public place or visible in your car.

USE travellers' cheques and credit cards rather than carrying much cash.

In case of loss or theft of Thomas Cook travellers' cheques, report to the Thomas Cook Refund Centre. A 24-hour emergency telephone number is provided on page 183. Emergency local assistance can also be obtained from Thomas Cook foreign exchange branches. A complete list of addresses can be found on page 190.

CHOOSE a money belt or bum bag rather than a handbag, but wear it in

On duty in downtown Miami

front. If you must carry a handbag, put it in front of you and keep a hand on it.

ONLY use bank teller machines in well-lit public areas.

NEVER hitch a lift, never pick up a hitchhiker. It is illegal as well as being dangerous.

NEVER wind your car window down if you are flagged down, unless by the police. Be careful if you stop to ask directions from a stranger.

If you are unlucky enough to be accosted, hand over your money. A few dollars is not worth the risk of physical violence.

CUSTOMS REGULATIONS

Hand your customs declaration form to Customs. It should list all things brought into the US, whether gifts for others or not. There is no limit to the amount of cash or American or foreign travellers' cheques you may bring in or take out. Not allowed: fresh meat, fruit, drugs (other than prescribed) and plants. Regulations are currently under review – check before leaving. However, current allows are as follows: allowances of duty frees are – over 21: 200 cigarettes and 100 cigars, and 1 litre of spirits. Over 17 but under 21: no spirits allowed.

DISABLED TRAVELLERS

You will invariably find ramps, wide doors, lifts and other wheelchair provisions in resort hotels, larger restaurants, theme parks and other popular areas. Some hotels have telephones specially designed for hearing-impaired people. Disabled people are officially referred to as being 'physically challenged'. *The Physically Challenged Guide to Florida* is a comprehensive brochure, listing names, addresses and phone numbers of organisations that can help the disabled traveller. It is available from the Florida Department of Commerce, Division of Tourism, Visitor Enquiry, 107 West Gaines Street, Collins Building, Tallahassee, FL 32399-2000. Tel: (904) 488-7598; fax (904) 487-1407.

Driving

Contact your car hire firm, either direct or through your travel agent for documentary proof of disabled driver status, such as the blue International Access Symbol. When you arrive, the car rental company will point you to the local county office to claim status as a disabled visitor. You may have to wait

Travel in style in a rented car

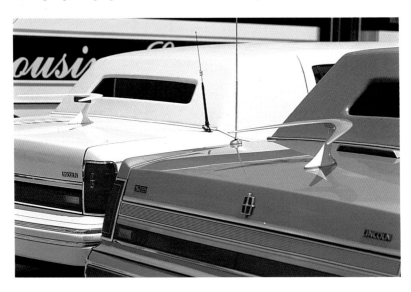

A Ford Thunderbird – highly collectable

up to 2 hours for a disabled visitor badge which gives some parking concessions. It may be worth using Orlando Airport because of a helpful organisation which will speed this and many matters: **Friends of the Family**, Suite 209, The Entertainment Complex, 1727 Orlando Central Parkway, Orlando, FL 33809. Tel: (407) 856–7676. Fax: (407) 856–7516. Contact them in advance.

DRIVING
Car hire
European nationals can drive in Florida on their own full driving licence and hire a car though an International Driving Permit may be useful. Under-25s may find hiring difficult or have to pay more for travel insurance (already high). Ask your travel agent about fly-drive schemes or booking before you leave home, as this may be cheaper than booking when in Florida. Take the booking form with you and present it to the car hire company (usually at or close to the airport). On top of this hire charge, you will be advised to take out Collision

Damage Waiver (CDW) insurance. It is expensive – around $10-12 a day – but essential as it covers you for every tiny scratch to your hire car, which would otherwise be charged to you, irrespective of whose fault it was. Almost all cars have automatic transmission, and all come with air-conditioning and an excellent stereo radio.

Most of the big hire companies are represented, usually based at airports, or with buses to take arriving passengers from the airport to a nearby car centre.

Petrol is basically very cheap, (lead-free is a little dearer). Some gas stations require you to pay before you fill up.

Roads and regulations
Drive on the right. If you feel nervous about driving on the right, it is worth making sure you arrive in daylight rather than tackle the first stretch in the dark. You will soon get used to it, but beware that you don't lose your concentration after stopping.

Types of road

Best for long-distance travel, but not sightseeing, are the Interstates (eg I-75). These have up to six lanes. Lane discipline is poor to non-existent. Americans overtake on both sides, a shock first time if you're in lane 3 between two jumbo trucks! US Highways (eg US 1) are much like a British dual carriageways. Don't be surprised at a parallel, scenic route, eg A1A, which runs along the seaward side (east) for most of the way (usually an older road superseded by the newer US Highway). These were often earlier State Routes or Highways, designated by the letters SR; many still are. The next category is County Roads (CR). The most noticeable toll road is Florida's Turnpike, over 300 miles north to south. On some toll roads you get a distance marker when you go on and pay as you leave. On others, you pre-pay by throwing a selection of small coins into a

basket. Tolls range from 25 cents to a few dollars. It is best to keep coins in the car, but don't panic if you don't have change, as attendants are always on hand. In towns, many roads have names as well as numbers, which sometimes change along their length.

Speed limits

The maximum speed is 65mph and the outer city limit, usually 55mph, starts far out. In built-up areas, it is 20–30mph (outside built-up areas 45mph). If the police stop you, wait in the car and be polite. Humour won't help. Speeding offences sometimes go to court and a base fine is $54, plus $4 for every mile over the limit. Alternatively you may be fined on the spot. Cities have good parking areas (often free) and parking meters – 25c to $1 an hour. Your wheelsmay be clamped for a parking

The Interstate into Orlando

offence, and a sticker tells you where to pay the $30 fine.

Drinking and driving
This is a serious offence and you can be locked up until you've taken a urine test, or lose your licence on the spot. The best advice is don't drink and drive. Any alcohol carried in a car must be unopened and be in the boot.

Highway breakdown
Emergency phones are situated only in official off-road parking. Wait with your vehicle, with the bonnet raised until the Highway Patrol stop to help you otherwise call the all-America helpline on 1–800–336–HELP. If your hire car breaks down, phone the number on the dashboard sticker.

ELECTRICITY
The standard electricity supply is 110 volts (60 cycles). You may have to bring an adaptor to convert. Sockets take plugs with two flat pins.

EMERGENCIES AND EMERGENCY PHONE NUMBERS
Fire, police, ambulance
In an emergency, phone 911, then ask for police, fire, or ambulance.

The driver of this Peterbilt truck takes a roadside breather

Money
Most banks and issuers of travellers' cheques (and credit cards) give an emergency number to report thefts. Make sure you have a note of these (and cheque numbers) before you leave and keep them separately from your cheques. Report losses to the police, and to these numbers:

Thomas Cook travellers' cheque refund: (1–800) 223–7373.
Visa: (1–800) 627–6811 or (1–800) 227–6811.
American Express Travellers' Cheques:
Credit cards: (1–800) 528–2121. Diners Card: (1–800) 068–8300.
Access/MasterCard: Issuing bank's emergency number.

Doctors, Dentists
Numbers are given in the Yellow Pages, under Dentists, Physicians and Surgeons, or Clinics, or phone the local casualty hospital.

The range of toy shops available is vast

HEALTH

From Europe, no inoculations are mandatory, and no special precautions are needed. Water is safe to drink though heavily chlorinated. Many drugs not on prescription in Europe need one in America. For minor ailments, use a drugstore's pharmacy section. Be sure to use a good sunscreen or blocker. A sun hat is also recommended. Carry insect repellent and soothing cream, particularly if you are venturing to the Everglades.

INSURANCE AND SAFETY

Health insurance is essential because medical attention is very expensive. A consultation (pre-paid) costs from $50 to $70, and medicine is pricey. Keep all medical receipts, loss details, and any police data to assist your insurance claim.

LOST PROPERTY

There is no central lost property depot. If you leave something on the plane, consult the airline at the arrival airport.

MAPS

Florida's Official Transportation Map is adequate for driving, and also gives selected city details. Available from the Florida Department of Commerce, 107 West Gaines Street, Collins Building, Tallahassee, FL 32399-2000, or larger Tourist Information Offices or Visitor and Convention Bureaux. There are several commercial maps available in shops and visitor centres. Most areas print their own and there will be maps of varying standard in a tourist brochure.

MEDIA

Newspapers

The three biggest dailies are the *Miami Herald*, the *Orlando Sentinel* and the *Tampa Tribune,* but each area will have its own. Don't miss the Sunday editions, which give comprehensive listings of arts, entertainment, food and drinking establishments. British, European and other overseas newspapers are scarce outside Orlando. Ask your hotel for the nearest stockist. Freesheets are useful for local happenings, and good for finding the night life and local hostelries.

Papers and *TV Guide* provide all broadcasting details.

Television

There are many local stations, while major networks (ABC, CBS and NBC) and their local affiliates offer national and international news. Early and late evenings are the main slots. Despite their status, news is heavy on trivia and is very parochial. To get away from the commercials tune into the PBS (Public Broadcasting Service) channel.

Radio
Changing radio channels provides interest because of the sheer diversity, from fire and brimstone to endless pop and rock. Try the public service channels and also some good college channels. These are mostly on FM. Serious talk radio has largely died out in the US.

MONEY MATTERS
America functions largely on plastic money, and Florida is no exception. Thomas Cook travellers' cheques should be carried in US dollars. These are accepted as cash in hotels, restaurants, gas stations and larger shops and change is given as appropriate without any extra commission charged. A complete list of Thomas Cook foreign exchange branches can be found on page 190.

In practice you will therefore never need to change money at a bank. Best accepted cards are MasterCard, American Express and Visa. You may be asked to show, or give an imprint of, the card as you check in at a hotel.

Tax
Everything you buy includes six per cent state sales tax, generally not shown on the price tickets.

OPEN SEASONS
With both summer and winter seasons, Florida is open all year round, though some swimming attractions close in winter. In summer the hotels are full of overseas visitors. In winter (high season), Florida attracts thousands from the cold north of America. Some beach resorts are packed with students for the spring break.

Newspaper vending machines

OPENING HOURS

Shops: general shop hours are 9–10am to 6–8pm, Monday to Saturday. In practice it is always possible to find somewhere open in cities, and many shopping complexes open Sundays.

Banks: generally 10am–3pm, Monday to Friday, till 6pm on either Thursdays or Fridays.

ORGANISED TOURS

Every Visitor and Convention Bureau will have lists of organised tours including cruises. See also **What to See** sections.

Stars and stripes decorate a mailbox

PLACES OF WORSHIP

All main cities will have Christian churches (of many denominations) and Jewish places of worship. Ask at your local Visitor and Convention Bureau or Tourist Office for details.

POLICE

City police patrol the streets and will give advice and help if asked politely. Traffic police, who patrol the roads and give tickets for speeding, are called the Highway Patrol ('State Troopers'). In an emergency dial 911, then ask for Police. Look up the local police number in the telephone directory.

POST (MAIL)

Hours are usually Monday to Friday 9am–6pm, Saturday 8/9am–noon. Offices have outside mailboxes, and similar boxes (blue) are set at many street corners.

Stamps are available from almost anywhere, even the supermarket. Postcards to Europe take a week to 10 days. Always use the zip code for American addresses.

Poste restante

Called General Delivery, post offices hold letters for 30 days. Letters must include the post office's zip code. Take identification with you to claim.

Telegrams (wires)

Western Union and International Telephone and Telegraph (ITT) take wires by phone. Check the local phone book or call the operator for the toll-free numbers of their offices.

PUBLIC HOLIDAYS

1 January – New Year's Day
15 January – Martin Luther King Day

Plymouth Congregational Church in Miami. Main towns usually have places of worship to suit all denominations

3rd Monday in February –
    Washington's Birthday
last Monday in May – Memorial Day
4 July – Independence Day
1st Monday in September – Labor Day
2nd Monday in October –
    Columbus Day
11 November – Veterans' Day
4th Thursday in November –
    Thanksgiving Day
25 December – Christmas Day

PUBLIC TRANSPORT
Airlines
If you plan to travel much by air in Florida, explore airpass schemes which most US airlines offer before you leave. Once there, look for offers in newspapers and phone the airlines:

American: (1–800) 433–7300;
British Airways: (1–800) AIRWAYS;
Continental: (1–800) 525–0280;
Delta Airlines: (1–800) 221–1212;
NorthWest: (1–800) 447–4747;
USAir: (1–800) 428–4322.

Train
See **Getting Around** (page 16–17).

Bus
See the phone books for the local office. For advice before you leave, or to buy a Greyhound Ameripass, phone the Greyhound Office at 342–117317, or branches of Thomas Cook. See page 17.

On the crest of a wave ...

SENIOR CITIZENS

Florida has more 'seniors' among its population and visitors than any other US state but, like most of America, does not easily admit to the fact of ageing.

Many discounts and 'extras' are available to senior citizens aged 55 and over, particularly on off-peak travel, some accommodation and entrance fees. Senior citizen prices will often be listed at ticket offices, and shown on advertisements, but always ask about discounts in case they are being coy. Also consult your travel agent about seniors' discounts.

SPORTS

Participant sports, see pages 158–61. Spectator sports, see pages 164–5.

STUDENT AND YOUTH TRAVEL

Some tour operators specialise in travel for young people and/or exchange programmes. Florida has few youth hostels. Some museums, galleries and attractions will offer student discounts. Always ask.

TELEPHONES

Several Florida companies link into the AT&T network. Sometimes, on official numbers, a mechanical voice answers and gives you a couple of further digits to push for a variety of services.

Public phones use 25c, 10c and 5c coins, and are located in hotel and other lobbies, train and bus stations, airports, bars and restaurants.

Florida is divided into four area codes: 305, 407, 813 and 904. Charges vary.

A local call (no area code needed) is cheap, 20c for the first 3 minutes. For a zone call (within the area but long-distance) dial 1 plus the phone number (no area code). US long-distance is costly. Dial 1+ area code + phone number. Always have plenty of change ready to put in when a voice (operator or mechanical) gives the instruction. Cheaper rates run between 5pm and 11pm, with the cheapest rates between 11pm and 8am.

For international calls direct, dial 011 + country code + number. Country codes: from US to Britain 44; Ireland 353; Australia 61; New Zealand 64; and Canada 1.

For the international operator, dial (1-800) 874–4000. Calls from hotel rooms attract a hefty premium. You can reverse charges – called 'collect' (for which the person called is asked to pay) – by dialling 0 + 1 + area code and number.

Many offices and public places have toll-free (freephone) lines, prefixed by 800 or 1–800, followed by a number, or letter sequence. eg (1–800) WDISNEY. The 800 numbers apply only inside the US.

TIME

Most of Florida is on Eastern Standard Time, which varies from:
Britain and Ireland – minus 5 hours
Western Europe   minus 6 hours
Australia – minus 15 hours
New Zealand – minus 17 hours

Florida also has US Daylight Saving Time (clocks move forward one hour) from the first Sunday in April to the last Sunday in October.

The Panhandle, west of the Apalachicola River, uses Central Standard Time, one hour behind the rest of Florida.

TIPPING

Employers take it for granted that you will tip waiters, cloakroom attendants,

Waiters rely on tips to supplement their wages, which are not generally high

etc, in Florida and reflect it in the wages they offer. Most hotels do not include a service charge. Tipping is, therefore, universal for hotel bellhops, doormen and airport porters at, at least, 50c a bag, ($1 a bag in a smart hotel), and for chambermaids at $2 a night. Taxi drivers, waiters/waitresses and hairdressers expect at least 15 per cent. If you pay by credit card, add the tip to the total before filling in the form and signing it.

TOILETS

These are found in airports and train and bus stations. All have good-quality lavatory and washing facilities. Cities do not provide 'public' toilets as such. Most people use the facilities in bars, restaurants and filling stations. Colloquially a toilet is called a 'john'.

TOURISM OFFICES

The Florida Division of Tourism operates visitor centres in major towns and resorts. For information on the state contact the office at 107 West Gaines Street, Collins Building, Tallahassee, FL 32399–2000. Tel: (904) 488–7598.

Regional Tourism Offices

Destination Daytona 126 E Orange Avenue, PO Box 910, Daytona Beach, FL 32115. Tel: (904) 255–0415.

Florida Keys and Key West Visitors Bureau, PO Box 114–7, Key West, FL 33041. Tel: (305) 296–3811.

Greater Fort Lauderdale Convention and Visitors Bureau, 200 East Las Olas Boulevard, Suite 1500, Fort Lauderdale FL 33301. Tel: (305) 765–4466.

Greater Miami Convention and Visitors Bureau, 701 Brickell Avenue, Suite 2700, Miami, FL 33131. Tel: (305) 539–3000.

Kissimmee St Cloud Convention and Visitors Bureau, PO Box 422007, Kissimmee, FL 34742–2007. Tel: (407) 847–5000.

Lee County Convention and Visitors Bureau, PO Box 2445, Fort Myers, FL 33902. Tel: (813) 335–2631.

Marco Island Convention and Visitors Bureau, 1102 North Collier Boulevard, Marco Island, FL 33937. Tel: (813) 394–7509.

Orlando/Orange County Convention and Visitors Bureau, 7208 Sand Lake Road, Suite 300, Orlando, FL 32819. Tel: (407) 363–5800.

Palm Beach County Convention and Visitors Bureau, 1555 Palm Beach Lakes Boulevard, Suite 204, West Palm Beach, FL 33401. Tel: (407) 471–3995.

Pensacola Convention and Visitor Information Center 1401 E Gregory Street, Pensacola, FL 32501. Tel: (904) 434–1234.

Pinellas County Tourist Development Council, Florida Suncoast Dome, One Stadium Drive, Suite A, St Petersburg FL 33705. Tel: (813) 892–7892.

St Augustine/St John's County Chamber of Commerce 1 Riberia Street, St Augustine, FL 32084. Tel: (904) 829–5681.

Tallahassee Area Convention and Visitors Bureau 200 West College Avenue, Tallahassee, FL 32302. Tel: (904) 651–7160.

Tampa/Hillsborough Convention and Visitors Association, 111 Madison Street, Suite 1010, Tampa, FL 33602. Tel: (813) 826–8358.

Thomas Cook Foreign Exchange Branches

3526 North Ocean Boulevard, Fort Lauderdale.

155 Southeast Third Avenue, Miami.

Fontainebleau Hotel, 4441 Collins Avenue, Miami Beach.

1751 Hotel Plaza Boulevard, Lake Buena Vista.

Clarion Plaza Hotel, 9700 International Drive, Orlando.

Marriott World Center, 8701 World Center Drive, Orlando.

5750 Major Boulevard, Suite 100, Orlando.

Quality Inn Plaza, 9000 International Drive, Orlando.

ACKNOWLEDGEMENTS
The Automobile Association would like to thank the following photographers, libraries and associations for their assistance in the preparation of this book.

Pete Bennett was commissioned to take photographs not listed below.

ALACHUA C & VB 140 189 114, 157 171 56 FLORIDA DEPARTMENT OF TOURISM 20b, 125, 133, 137, 160, 161, 163b, 165, 166, 188 FLORIDA PINELLAS SUNCOAST 79c, 167 GEIGER & ASSOCIATES 59, 60, 61 GREATER MIAMI C & VB 72, 73c, 74, 75, 76, 82, 99c, 154, 155 JACKSONVILLE CONVENTION BUREAU 99b KENNEDY SPACE CENTER 58 KISSIMMEE – ST CLOUD C & VB 151 LEE COUNTY C & VB 102 NATURE PHOTOGRAPHERS LTD 20a (K J Carson), 21a (P R Sterry), 21b (W S Paton), 49 (S C Bisserot), 141 (P R Sterry), 142 (P R Sterry), 143a (E A Janes), 143b (A J Cleave), 143 c (P R Sterry), 143d (P R Sterry) NORTHWEST AIRLINES 176 ORLANDO C & VB 39a, 39b, 45, 175a, 175b POLK COUNTY C & VB 158, 162b, 164 ROBINSON & ST JOHN 41 ST AUGUSTINE CHAMBER OF COMMERCE 23, 98, 99a, 125b, 125c, 159a SARASOTA C & VB 150 SEA WORLD 50 SPECTRUM COLOUR LIBRARY 7, 57, 73a, 123b, 124, 159b, 185 WALT DISNEY COMPANY (copyright) 46, 47a, 47b, 173, 174 ZEFA PICTURE LIBRARY 73b ZIMMERMAN AGENCY 131, 162a

The author wishes to thank the following for their help: Rachel O'Connor, Florida Division of Tourism in London; John Rutherford, Orlando; Brenda Roth, St Augustine; Georgia Carter, Daytona Beach; Wes Biggs, Florida Nature Tours, and David Rose of Northwest Airlines.

CONTRIBUTORS
Series Adviser: Melissa Shales **Copy Editor:** Paul Murphy **Indexer:** Marie Lorimer